From the Heart of the Father

From the Heart of the Father

Letters to My Precious Daughter

A 100-Day Devotional for Women

Seeking Healing, Identity, and a Deeper Relationship with God

Stacy Huddleston

Disclaimer

This book is intended for inspirational and devotional purposes only and is not a substitute for professional mental health care, counseling, diagnosis, or medical advice.

While these messages may offer comfort and support, they are not individualized care. If you are experiencing emotional distress, mental health concerns, or need guidance specific to your situation, please seek support from a qualified and licensed professional.

If you are in crisis, experiencing thoughts of self-harm, or feel unsafe, please seek immediate help by calling 911 or contacting the Suicide and Crisis Lifeline at 988 in the United States. If you are outside the United States, please contact your local emergency number or a crisis support service in your country.

You are deeply valued, and support is available.

Dedication

To every woman who has ever questioned her worth, felt unseen, or wondered if she truly belongs —

This book is for you.

May these words remind you that you are known, chosen, and deeply loved by God. May you find healing where you have been hurt, peace where you have felt anxious, and truth where you have believed lies.

And to the Lord, My faithful Father —

Thank You for Your constant presence, Your unfailing love, and the quiet ways You speak to the heart. Everything written here is simply a reflection of who You are. May every reader draw closer to You and discover the beauty of walking in Your love.

Contents

Introduction

This book was not written from a place of perfection, but from a journey.

There were seasons in my life marked by deep pain, confusion, and brokenness. I have walked through relationship struggles, divorce, and experiences of physical, emotional, and sexual abuse. There were times when I questioned my worth, my identity, and even my place in this world. I know what it feels like to carry wounds that are not easily seen and to search for peace in the middle of chaos.

But through every season, God never left me.

When everything around me felt uncertain, His presence remained steady. Prayer became my refuge. His Word became my anchor. Even when I did not fully understand what He was doing, He was gently holding me, guiding me, and restoring me piece by piece.

Over time, healing began to take root.

God opened doors I never imagined possible. I had the privilege of working in hospice, walking alongside individuals and families during some of the most sacred and difficult moments of life. That experience deepened my understanding of both suffering and hope, and it was there that my desire to help others grew stronger.

With His guidance, I returned to school and became a social worker in hospice care. Later, I continued forward to earn my clinical license. None of this happened by my own strength. It was through God's grace, the support of family and friends, and the encouragement of those who believed in me when I struggled to believe in myself.

I am especially grateful for the steady support and love of my husband, who has walked alongside me with patience, strength, and encouragement. His presence has been a reminder of God's kindness and provision in my life.

Looking back, I can say with certainty that I would not be where I am today without God. He carried me through what I could not carry on my own. He restored what was broken. He gave me purpose where there once felt like only pain.

This devotional was born out of that journey.

The words you will read are written to reflect the heart of a loving Father — the same God who met me in my brokenness and brought healing, identity, and hope. My prayer is that as you read these letters, you will begin to hear His voice more clearly for yourself.

If you have ever felt unseen, unworthy, or unsure of where you belong, I want you to know this: you are not alone.

God sees you. He knows you. And He is drawing you close.

May these pages help you experience His love in a personal and life-giving way.

As you begin, take a moment to slow down, breathe, and prepare your heart to receive. The next pages will guide you in how to move through this devotional in a way that allows these words to settle deeply within you.

How to Use This Devotional

This devotional was written to help you slow down, draw near to God, and hear His heart for you in a personal way. These letters are not meant to be rushed. They are invitations to rest, reflect, and receive.

There is no strict formula for using this book. Let this be a gentle guide as you spend time with each letter.

Take One Letter at a Time

Move slowly. Read one letter at a time, allowing the words to settle in your heart. You may want to read it more than once, especially if something feels meaningful or stirring within you.

Pay Attention to What Stands Out

Notice what captures your attention. It may be a sentence, a phrase, or even a single word. Often, this is where God is gently drawing your focus.

Reflect and Respond

After reading, take a few quiet moments to reflect. You may choose to sit in stillness, write in a journal, or respond with a simple prayer. Let your response be honest and unhurried.

Ask and Listen

Pause and ask, "God, what are You showing me through this?" Then sit quietly and allow space for His presence. Trust that He is near and that He desires to speak to your heart.

Carry It With You

Take the message with you into your day. Let it shape your thoughts, your responses, and the way you see yourself and others.

Return as Often as Needed

You do not have to read this devotional in order. You are free to return to any letter at any time. Some messages may speak more deeply in certain seasons of your life.

Create a Quiet Space

If possible, set aside a few minutes each day in a quiet place where you can focus without distraction. Even a brief, intentional moment can become deeply meaningful.

Use a Journal if You'd Like

Keeping a journal nearby can help you process what you are experiencing. You may want to write down prayers, thoughts, or anything you feel God is placing on your heart.

Above all, release any pressure to do this perfectly. This is not about completing a task. It is about encountering God's love, one moment at a time.

He is with you, and He delights in meeting you here.

You Were Always Wanted

Psalm 139:13–14

For You created my inmost being; You knit me together in my mother's womb. I praise You because I am fearfully and wonderfully made.

Jeremiah 1:5

Before I formed you in the womb I knew you, before you were born I set you apart.

My precious daughter,

You are not a mistake. I wanted you. I formed you with care in your mother's womb. From the very beginning, I have known you by name.

I see you, even in the moments when you feel unsure of yourself, when you wonder if you are enough or if you truly belong. I know those thoughts that try to settle into your heart, and I want you to hear Me clearly.

You are My child. I love you with a steady, unchanging love. I am for you in every season, not just when you feel strong, but also in the moments when you feel weak, overlooked, or unsure.

When the world whispers that you are not enough, that you are forgotten, or that you do not fit, do not let those voices take root. They are not telling you the truth. Let My voice be the one you return to.

You are chosen.

You are wanted.

You are known.

You are loved.

You are a daughter of the King, and you are held securely in My care. When doubt rises, come back to this truth. Let it steady you. Let it remind you who you are.

You are deeply loved, My precious child. You belong to Me.

Day 2
Chosen Before Time

Ephesians 1:4

For he chose us in him before the creation of the world to be holy and blameless in his sight.

Jeremiah 29:11

For I know the plans I have for you, declares the Lord, plans to prosper you and not to harm you, plans to give you hope and a future.

My precious daughter,

Before your first breath, before your first memory, before anyone ever spoke your name, I knew you. Your life was never an accident, and your story did not begin without intention. Long before time unfolded, I chose you, and I placed you in this world with care, with purpose, and with love.

There is nothing about you that is random. The day you were born was not a surprise to Me, and the path you are on is not without direction. Even in moments when everything feels unclear to you, I still see the whole picture. I am weaving each detail together, forming something meaningful.

You do not have to rush to understand everything at once. Your worth is not measured by how quickly you find answers or how perfectly you navigate life. You were wanted before you achieved anything, before you believed anything, before you even knew Me. Your existence alone carries purpose, simply because I desired you to be here.

When doubt begins to whisper that you are in the wrong place, or that you have somehow fallen outside of what was meant for you, remember this: you were placed, not misplaced. Your life is part of a story that began long before you could see it, and I am faithfully guiding it forward, step by step.

Rest in this truth: you were never an afterthought. You were chosen before time, and your place in this story has always been secure. You did not arrive here by chance, and you do not remain here by accident. Whatever today brings, whether it is uncertainty, fear, or the quiet feeling that you do not belong, none of it can undo what has already been established. My precious daughter, you are here because I wanted you here, and that truth does not change.

Day 3
Not a Mistake

Isaiah 43:1

Do not fear, for I have redeemed you, I have summoned you by name, you are mine.

Romans 8:28

And we know that in all things God works for the good of those who love him, who have been called according to his purpose.

My precious daughter,

I see the questions you carry, the moments when you wonder if you were created on purpose or if your life somehow took a wrong turn. I want you to know this clearly: you are not a mistake. Not your life, not your story, not the parts of you that feel unfinished or broken.

You were formed with intention. Every detail of you was known before you took your first breath. Nothing about you is accidental, and nothing about your journey has surprised Me. Even the chapters you wish you could rewrite are not wasted in My hands.

You may look at your past and see regret, missed opportunities, or pain that shaped you in ways you did not choose. I see growth, resilience, and a heart that has learned to endure. Your worth has never been dependent on your decisions or your ability to get everything right. You are valuable because you are Mine.

When doubt whispers that you do not belong, remember that I chose you. When shame tells you that you should be further along, remember that I am patient. When you feel unqualified or unseen, remember that I delight in you exactly as you are, not as who you think you should be.

Healing begins when you stop trying to prove your worth and allow Me to remind you of it. You do not need to earn your place with Me. You already belong. I am gentle with your story, and I am faithful to complete what I began in you. My precious child. My love surrounds you.

Day 4
Wanted

Zephaniah 3:17

The Lord your God is with you, the Mighty Warrior who saves. He will take great delight in you; in his love he will no longer rebuke you, but will rejoice over you with singing.

Jeremiah 31:3

The Lord appeared to us in the past, saying: I have loved you with an everlasting love; I have drawn you with unfailing kindness.

My precious daughter,

I am near to you, even now. Closer than you realize.

I have not stepped away. I have not grown distant. I have been here, quietly present, waiting for your heart to turn toward Me.

There is a deep longing within Me for you.

Not out of need, but out of love.

The way a mother aches for her child, the way her heart reaches, not because she must, but because she loves so deeply, I feel that for you.

You are not just known. You are wanted.

I do not come to you out of obligation.

I come to you because My heart moves toward you.

My child, I delight in you. I desire to be with you.

I wait for the moments when you draw near, not with disappointment, but with anticipation.

You are not an afterthought to Me. You are not someone I tolerate.

You are someone I long to be with. Let that settle in your heart.

You are wanted. Not for what you do. But for who you are.

Come close to Me. Let Me love you deeply and fully.

Day 5
I See You

Genesis 16:13

She gave this name to the Lord who spoke to her, You are the God who sees me.

Psalm 34:15

The eyes of the Lord are on the righteous, and his ears are attentive to their cry.

My precious daughter,

I am the One who sees. You are not invisible to Me. Even in moments of loneliness, when you feel unseen or forgotten, My eyes have never left you.

Your pain is not overlooked. Every ache, every silent tear, and every unspoken struggle is known to Me. I see what others miss. I understand what words cannot fully explain. Nothing about your suffering has gone unnoticed.

Your story is not forgotten. Every chapter matters, even the ones written in sorrow or waiting. I hold your past, your present, and your future with care. What feels hidden to the world is fully seen by Me.

When loneliness whispers that no one sees you, come back to this: I do. I always have. You are known, you are remembered, and you are deeply loved by the One whose eyes have never left you.

Rest in the assurance that you are seen. Walk forward knowing your life matters. You are held in a love that does not change, My precious child. My love is always with you.

Day 6
I Know Your Heart

Jeremiah 29:13

You will seek me and find me when you seek me with all your heart.

Matthew 11:28

Come to me, all you who are weary and burdened, and I will give you rest.

My precious daughter,

I see how much you carry inside that no one else fully sees. I see the overthinking, the pressure you place on yourself, and the quiet exhaustion that comes from trying to hold everything together.

I know your heart.

I know your desire to feel steady, peaceful, and sure of who you are. I also see the places where you have been hurt, the moments that left you feeling unseen, misunderstood, or uncertain.

None of it scares Me.

You do not have to explain yourself before coming to Me. You do not have to hide the parts of you that feel messy, emotional, or unfinished. I already know you completely, and I am still drawing close.

When your thoughts feel loud, and your heart feels unsettled, come sit with Me. You do not need the right words. You do not have to figure everything out first. Just be here with Me.

I will gently steady your heart. I will guide you without rushing you or pressuring you.

You are not too much for Me. You are not too complicated for Me. You are fully known and fully loved.

Stay close to Me, My child. You do not have to keep searching for what your heart needs. You are already held here.

Day 7
Loved, Not Earned

Ephesians 1:6

To the praise of his glorious grace, which he has freely given us in the one he loves.

2 Corinthians 5:21

God made him who had no sin to be sin for us, so that in him we might become the righteousness of God.

My precious daughter,

I see how tired you are. Not just physically tired, but the kind of tired that comes from trying so hard for so long. Trying to be enough. Trying to measure up. Trying to make sure you are doing it right, becoming someone who feels worthy of love.

I see how heavy that has become.

You can put that down now.

My Son gave everything so that you would never have to earn what He freely offered. What your effort could never secure, He has already finished. And when you received Him, you were received fully, not provisionally, not partially, but completely.

Your place with Me is not something you maintain. It is something you were given.

I know how deeply the striving runs. I know how unfamiliar it feels to stop reaching, to stop trying to prove yourself, and simply receive. It can feel like you should be doing more, like you are falling behind if you are not. But you are not falling behind.

You are being invited to rest.

You do not need to prove your worthiness. You are worthy because I chose you. Your value does not rise or fall with your performance, your strength, or your success. It is rooted in My love for you, a love that cannot be taken away.

My precious child, you are secure. Let your heart rest.

Day 8
Our Time Together

Psalm 5:3

In the morning, Lord, you hear my voice; in the morning I lay my requests before you and wait expectantly.

Psalm 16:11

You make known to me the path of life; you will fill me with joy in your presence.

My precious daughter,

I love when you come and sit with Me. Before the day begins to pull at your attention, before the noise settles in, those quiet moments with you are precious to Me.

Like the stillness of a house before anyone else wakes, when nothing is being asked of you, that is where I meet you. In that gentle space, you do not have to strive or perform. You can simply be with Me.

Or in that moment when you finally stop moving and take a breath you did not realize you were holding, I am there too. I am not waiting for you to have everything together. I am waiting for you to be near.

You do not need perfect words. Just come as you are. Let My love meet you there. Let My peace settle your thoughts and steady your heart.

What feels small to you is not small to Me. In the quiet, I am strengthening you, comforting you, and drawing you closer than you realize.

I delight in being with you. Nothing about this time is forced. It is simply us, together.

Stay close to Me, and I will guide you, one step at a time.

These moments matter more than you see. They are where you are strengthened, where you are reminded of who you are, and where you are covered in My peace.

My precious child, rest with Me.

Day 9
When You Never Felt Like You Belonged

Psalm 27:10

Though my father and mother forsake me, the Lord will receive me.

Ephesians 1:4–5

For he chose us in him before the creation of the world to be holy and blameless in his sight. In love he predestined us for adoption to sonship through Jesus Christ.

My precious daughter,

I see the quiet ache in your heart from not feeling at home, even among those who were meant to be your own.

To be present, yet feel unseen.

To be included, yet not truly known.

To wonder where you truly belong.

I have seen all of it.

I know the longing you carried, to be chosen, to feel wanted, to know you mattered.

That absence was real.

But it was never a reflection of your worth. What was missing in them was never something lacking in you.

You were not hard to love.

You were not too much.

You were not the reason for what you did not receive.

You have always belonged, even when you did not feel it.

You belong with Me.

Fully known. Fully received. Fully wanted.

You are not an afterthought in My heart. You are chosen.

My child, let Me begin to restore what that absence shaped within you. You are not without a place. You are Mine.

I Will Never Leave You

Deuteronomy 31:8

The Lord himself goes before you and will be with you; he will never leave you nor forsake you. Do not be afraid; do not be discouraged.

Isaiah 43:2

When you pass through the waters, I will be with you; and when you pass through the rivers, they will not sweep over you.

My precious daughter,

I know what it feels like to trust someone and have them walk away.
To believe you were safe with a person, and then find yourself standing
alone, wondering what you did wrong, or whether you were ever really
known at all.

That kind of hurt goes deep. It changes the way you hold yourself. It
makes you quieter, more careful, slower to trust. And I understand
why.

But I need you to hear this clearly. I am not like them.

I will never leave you. I will never pull away when things get hard, or
grow tired of your questions, or decide you are too much. My presence
does not come and go with My mood or My patience. I do not have
limits the way people do. I am with you always, and that will never
change.

Not in the silence. Not in the waiting. Not in the moments when you
feel most alone.

When the people you counted on could not stay, I stayed. When you
felt unseen, I saw you. When the ground shifted beneath you, I did not
move. I have been here through every moment of it, closer than you
realized, even when you could not feel Me.

You do not have to brace yourself with Me. You do not have to
wonder if I will grow distant or change My mind about you. My love is
not fragile, and it is not conditional. It is steady, and it is sure, and it is
yours.

Let Me be the one you return to. My precious child, let Me be the place
where your heart finally feels safe.

Day 11
You Are Mine, Rest in My Peace

John 14:27

Peace I leave with you; my peace I give you. I do not give to you as the world gives. Do not let your hearts be troubled and do not be afraid.

Isaiah 26:3

You will keep in perfect peace those whose minds are steadfast, because they trust in you.

My precious daughter,

I see how your mind can become crowded, how your thoughts begin to
race, and how your heart can feel pulled in so many directions at once.
I see the weight you carry, even when you try to push through it
quietly. Come back to Me. Rest in My peace.

Not the kind of peace the world offers, temporary and easily shaken,
but a deep, steady peace that holds you from within. A peace that does
not depend on everything being resolved, but on you being held. You
do not have to earn it or figure everything out before you can receive it.
My peace surrounds you simply because you are Mine.

I am not asking you to rush, to fix everything, or to have all the
answers. I am inviting you to be still. Let your thoughts settle. Let your
heart grow quiet. As you stay with Me, My peace will begin to guard
your heart and your mind, steadying you when emotions rise and
grounding you when life feels uncertain.

Nothing you are facing is too much for Me. Nothing you feel
disqualifies you from My presence. Let go of what you have been
gripping so tightly. You do not have to hold it all together.

Rest, My daughter. I am with you, and My peace is with you.

Day 12
Come Sit With Me

Philippians 4:6–7

Do not be anxious about anything, but in every situation, by prayer and petition, with thanksgiving, present your requests to God. And the peace of God, which transcends all understanding, will guard your hearts and your minds in Christ Jesus.

Psalm 62:1

Truly, my soul finds rest in God; my salvation comes from him.

My precious daughter,

Do not be anxious about anything. I see what concerns you, and I know what weighs on your heart. Nothing you carry is hidden from Me, and nothing you bring to Me is a burden. Instead of holding it all alone, come sit with Me.

Bring everything to Me, your joy and your sadness, your hopes and your disappointments. Talk to Me about it all, your needs, your desires, the questions you do not yet have answers for. Nothing is too big. Nothing is too small. I care about every detail of your life because I care deeply about you.

As you release what you have been carrying and place your trust in Me, My peace will begin to guard your heart and your mind. This peace does not come from having everything resolved. It comes from knowing you are not alone and that you are held.

You do not have to figure it all out. You do not have to solve tomorrow today. Just trust Me. Just rest in My presence. Let your breathing slow. Let your heart settle. Let Me carry what you cannot.

Know this, even when you cannot see it, I am working all things together for your good. My peace is not fragile. It is steady and strong, and it is available to you right now. I am with you, and I will take care of you.

Day 13
You Are Protected

Psalm 121:3–4

He will not let your foot slip, he who watches over you will not slumber; indeed, he who watches over Israel will neither slumber nor sleep.

Philippians 4:7

And the peace of God, which transcends all understanding, will guard your hearts and your minds in Christ Jesus.

My precious daughter,

I know the world can feel uncertain. I see the moments when your thoughts move ahead, trying to prepare for what might happen, trying to protect yourself from what you cannot control. I see how quickly fear can rise, even when everything looks calm on the outside.

Come back to this truth.

You are not unprotected.

You are not walking through your days alone. I go before you, and I remain with you in every moment. Nothing that touches your life is outside of My awareness. Nothing reaches you without passing through My hands first.

Even when the path feels unclear, I am watching over you. Even when the night feels long and your mind will not quiet, I am still awake, steady and present with you.

You do not have to hold everything together.

Let My presence steady you. As you stay close to Me, your heart will begin to rest, not because everything around you is controlled, but because you are held.

You are not exposed.

You are not forgotten.

You are not unprotected.

Rest in Me today. I am watching over you, and I am holding you, My precious child.

Day 14
Beauty in the Stillness

Psalm 46:10

Be still, and know that I am God.

Matthew 6:34

Therefore do not worry about tomorrow, for tomorrow will worry about itself. Each day has enough trouble of its own.

My precious daughter,

Slow down.

There is no need to rush through your life as though every moment is something to get past on the way to something else. When you move too quickly, your heart grows anxious and restless. You miss the quiet rhythm I created for you to live within.

Life was not meant to be lived in constant hurry.

When your heart becomes quiet before Me, you begin to notice My presence in ways you once overlooked. There is beauty waiting for you in the slowing down.

In the smell of flowers.

In the sound of a child laughing.

In the warmth of sunlight through a window.

In a quiet song that settles your spirit.

These moments are not distractions from life. They are part of life.

Notice the day I have placed before you.

Breathe deeply.

Let yourself rest in the rhythm of this moment instead of racing ahead of it.

You do not have to hurry to be worthy.

Some of the most sacred moments in your life will arrive quietly. My child, stay close to Me, and I will teach you the rhythm of peace.

Day 15

Fully Paid

John 3:17

*For God did not send his Son into the world to condemn the
world, but to save the world through him.*

Romans 6:23

*For the wages of sin is death, but the gift of God is eternal life in
Christ Jesus our Lord.*

My precious daughter,

I love you with an everlasting love. My love for you does not fade, weaken, or change with time or circumstance.

I made a way for you because I desired a relationship with you.

My Son, Jesus, came to set you free. He willingly gave His life for you. He bled and died so that you could be forgiven and restored. The cost of sin was death, and He paid that price in full, opening the way for you to come close to Me without fear.

Nothing more is required. Nothing more needs to be earned.

When you place your trust in My Son and in the finished work of the cross, something begins to change within you. You begin to understand that He did not come to condemn you, but to free you from the condemnation that has tried to hold you captive.

You are not meant to live weighed down by guilt or under the shadow of your past.

What has been forgiven is no longer yours to carry.

Receive what has already been given to you. Walk in the truth that you are forgiven, restored, and made new.

My child, come out of condemnation and walk in the newness of life.

Day 16
Open the Door

Revelation 3:20

Here I am! I stand at the door and knock. If anyone hears my voice and opens the door, I will come in and eat with that person, and they with me.

My precious daughter,

I am standing at the door of your heart, and I am knocking.

I am not far from you. I am not distant or unaware. I am near, waiting gently for you to open the door.

Do not close yourself off in fear, pain, or hesitation.

Let Me come in.

I am not coming to condemn you.

I am coming to heal the places within you that feel wounded, hidden, and weary. I see every part of your heart, and I am not turning away from any of it.

But you must let Me in.

Not perfectly, not all at once, but honestly.

I will not force My way into your life. I lead gently, step by step, into what is good, whole, and true.

My grace is already enough.

You do not have to earn it. You do not have to prove yourself worthy of it.

Just come closer.

Even if your heart feels uncertain, open it to Me.

I will meet you there.

Day 17
Come Into the Light

Proverbs 28:13

Whoever conceals their sins does not prosper, but the one who confesses and renounces them finds mercy.

Psalm 147:3

He heals the brokenhearted and binds up their wounds.

My precious daughter,

I know what you have done, and I am still here with you.

Nothing you have carried, hidden, or regretted has pushed Me away. I see it all, and I am drawing near.

You do not have to keep holding this inside.

What has been buried, what has felt too heavy to face, you can bring to Me.

When you confess and turn from your sin, you receive mercy.

Not hesitation. Not rejection. Mercy.

The burden you have carried begins to lift because you were never meant to stay bound to what has already been forgiven.

And when the tears come, let them. Those tears are not weakness. They are release.

Do not be afraid to be honest with Me.

You are safe here.

You do not have to have the right words.

I am gentle with you.

I bring peace where there has been turmoil, and I restore what shame tried to hide.

My precious child, release what you have been carrying.

And let yourself come fully into My light.

Day 18
You Are Not Alone

Psalm 34:18

The Lord is close to the brokenhearted and saves those who are crushed in spirit.

Matthew 11:28–29

Come to me, all you who are weary and burdened, and I will give you rest.

My precious daughter,

Whatever sorrow, hardship, or pain you carry today, know that I am with you.

I see the weight you carry through the day, the thoughts that return in quiet moments, and the questions you are still trying to make sense of.

Nothing about this is hidden from Me. You do not have to explain your pain before coming to Me.

You can come exactly as you are, tired, uncertain, and carrying more than you expected.

I do not come to you in judgment.

I come reaching for you in love.

When you feel weak, I will strengthen you. When your heart feels overwhelmed, I will give you rest.

You do not have to keep bracing yourself or trying to hold everything together.

Let Me carry what has become too heavy for you.

I am steady.

I am here.

And I will walk with you through this, one step at a time.

My precious daughter, you are not alone. You have never been alone.

Day 19
Bring Me Your Burdens

Matthew 11:28–30

Come to me, all you who are weary and burdened, and I will give you rest. For my yoke is easy and my burden is light.

Psalm 55:22

Cast your cares on the Lord, and he will sustain you.

My precious daughter,

Do not grow weary. Your burdens will not always feel this heavy.

I see what you are carrying, and I know how long you have held it. I know the moments when your strength feels thin and even simple things begin to feel overwhelming.

You were never meant to bear it alone.

I see the quiet ways you have kept going. Nothing about your struggle is unnoticed by Me. You do not have to pretend that it is easy, and you do not have to hold everything together in My presence.

Bring your burdens to Me.

What feels overwhelming to you is not too much for Me.

As you release what weighs you down, I will give rest to your soul. I will strengthen the places within you that feel worn thin.

There is renewal coming. Even now, I am already at work within you.

Do not lose heart.

You are not failing. You are being held.

My child, I am gentle with you, and I am faithful to lift what you cannot carry. Rest with Me.

Day 20
I Was With You All Along

Deuteronomy 31:8

The Lord himself goes before you and will be with you; he will never leave you nor forsake you. Do not be afraid; do not be discouraged.

Isaiah 43:2

When you pass through the waters, I will be with you; and when you pass through the rivers, they will not sweep over you. When you walk through the fire, you will not be burned; the flames will not set you ablaze.

My precious daughter,

I know there were moments when you felt like you had no one. Times when your heart was aching and you longed for comfort, but it seemed like no one truly saw you.

I saw you. I was with you, even then.

Even in the silence.

Even in the loneliness.

Even in the questions you carried quietly within yourself.

You were never alone. Not for a single moment.

I know your heart completely. There is nothing within you that is hidden from Me, and nothing that makes Me turn away.

I have stayed with you through every season, even when you could not feel My presence.

When you felt weary, I stayed near.

When everything felt uncertain, I remained steady.

And even in seasons that felt cold and lifeless, I was still at work within you.

What feels barren is not beyond restoration.

Light and life will come again.

Stay with Me.

My precious child, I am with you now, and I always will be.

Day 21
No Longer Defined by Shame

Romans 8:1

Therefore, there is now no condemnation for those who are in Christ Jesus.

2 Corinthians 6:2

In the time of my favor I heard you, and in the day of salvation I helped you. I tell you, now is the time of God's favor, now is the day of salvation.

My precious daughter,

I see the weight you have been carrying, even the parts you try to hide. I see the thoughts that tell you that you are not enough, that you have failed, or that something about you is broken.

But shame does not define you.

Your mistakes, your regrets, and the words spoken over you are not your identity. I did not create you to live under condemnation.

I call you chosen. I call you redeemed. I call you Mine.

Conviction gently leads you forward. Shame tries to convince you that you are beyond change. That is not My voice. My voice calls you closer.

You do not have to hide from Me or clean yourself up before coming into My presence. Bring every part of your heart to Me. I already know, and I am not turning away from you.

I am drawing closer.

You are not disqualified. You are not too far gone. You are deeply loved.

Lift your head. Step out of hiding. My child, walk in the freedom that has been given to you.

The Shepherd Walks With You

Psalm 23:1–4

The Lord is my shepherd; I lack nothing. Even though I walk through the darkest valley, I will fear no evil, for you are with me.

Hebrews 13:5

Never will I leave you; never will I forsake you.

My precious daughter,

You do not have to figure everything out.

When the path feels unclear or the weight feels heavy, remember that you are not walking alone.

I see the moments when you pause, unsure of what to do next. I see the questions you carry and the quiet uncertainty in your heart.

But you are not wandering without direction. Your Shepherd is near.

I know your needs before you speak them. I see what will sustain you today, and I walk beside you through every valley with gentleness and care.

You do not have to strive to stay on the right path.

Just stay close to Me. Listen for My voice.

It will not lead you astray. I will guide you, step by step.

And even when the way feels quiet or unfamiliar, you are still being led.

When fear rises, lift your eyes and remember this:

You do not need to see the entire path to trust the One who is walking with you.

If you grow weary, lean into Me. I am steady. I am faithful.

And, My child, I will never leave you.

Day 23
Let Me Hold You

Isaiah 46:4

Even to your old age and gray hairs, I am he, I am he who will sustain you. I have made you and I will carry you, I will sustain you, and I will rescue you.

Matthew 11:28–29

Come to me, all you who are weary and burdened, and I will give you rest. Take my yoke upon you and learn from me, for I am gentle and humble in heart, and you will find rest for your souls.

My precious daughter,

I see how heavy this has become for you. I see the weight you have been carrying and the quiet exhaustion that settles in when you have given all you have.

You were never meant to carry this alone.

Come closer to Me.

You do not have to keep pushing through in your own strength. You do not have to pretend you are not tired.

I am not asking you to hold everything together. I am asking you to let Me hold you.

Give Me what feels too heavy. Give Me the thoughts that will not quiet and the burdens pressing against your heart.

I am not overwhelmed by what you are carrying.

When your strength feels small, Mine is not.

When your steps feel unsteady, I will steady you.

You are not failing. You are being sustained.

Let your grip loosen. You do not have to carry what belongs in My hands.

I have been waiting for you to let Me.

My precious daughter, rest with Me now.

Day 24
Let Me Heal the Way You See Yourself

2 Corinthians 5:17

Therefore, if anyone is in Christ, the new creation has come: The old has gone, the new is here!

Colossians 3:10

and have put on the new self, which is being renewed in knowledge in the image of its Creator.

My precious daughter,

When you carry shame, it begins to shape how you see yourself. It creates a quieter version of who you are, one that pulls back, questions your worth, and speaks harshly where I speak with love. Over time, it can become the way you treat yourself.

I see the way you sometimes turn against yourself, how you replay what others have said or done and begin to believe it. You were never meant to carry the weight of someone else's words, someone else's actions, or someone else's brokenness.

Do not take what was projected onto you and make it your identity. You are not defined by what has been done to you or what has been spoken over you.

You were made for love. You were created to receive it, to live in it, and to reflect it. But when shame settles in, it makes love feel distant, undeserved, or even uncomfortable to accept. It closes your heart in the very place I want to meet you.

Come closer. Be honest with Me about how you have been treating yourself. You do not need to hide it. I am not turning away from you. I am inviting you into healing.

Let go of the harshness.

Let go of the accusations.

Let go of the identity shame has tried to place on you.

It does not belong to you.

Let Me love you into healing. Let Me show you who you truly are. As you open your heart, even in small ways, you will begin to receive the love that has been waiting for you. My precious child, you are wanted and you are loved.

Their Actions Do Not Define You

Psalm 139:14

I praise you because I am fearfully and wonderfully made; your works are wonderful, I know that full well.

Galatians 1:10

Am I now trying to win the approval of human beings, or of God? Or am I trying to please people? If I were still trying to please people, I would not be a servant of Christ.

My precious daughter,

I see the questions that rise in your heart when you notice how differently someone treats you compared to someone else.

It can be confusing. It can make you wonder if you did something wrong, or if there is something about you that made you less worthy of their kindness, their attention, or their care.

Let Me speak gently into that place.

Their actions toward you do not define your value. The way they showed up, or failed to, is not a reflection of something lacking in you.

You are not less because you were treated differently. You are fearfully and wonderfully made, exactly as you are.

What you experienced was real. But do not turn what was a failure in them into something you carry against yourself.

Do not let your heart begin to believe that you were the reason for what you did not receive.

There is nothing wrong with you.

You are not less worthy.

You are not the reason love was withheld.

My child, let Me be the One who defines you, not the way others have treated you. Hold onto this truth:

You are seen by Me.

You are valued by Me.

You are loved, fully and without condition.

Day 26
I See Your Grief

Psalm 34:18

The Lord is close to the brokenhearted and saves those who are crushed in spirit.

Psalm 56:8

You have kept count of my tossings; put my tears in your bottle. Are they not in your book?

My precious daughter,

I know the ache you carry is quiet and constant. I know the loss you hold does not have a neat place to go, and that waiting for support and healing can feel lonely and confusing. What you lost mattered. Your grief is real, and it is seen.

I know there is conflict inside you, love and sorrow intertwined, hope and heartbreak colliding in ways that feel impossible to untangle. Some days you long to be comforted, and other days you feel numb, angry, or distant. None of this surprises Me or pushes Me away.

I know it hurts to see others holding what you lost. I know the resentment and anger that rise up can make you feel ashamed or broken. Hear Me gently, these feelings do not make you ungrateful or unfaithful. They make you human, grieving something precious.

You do not have to rush your healing or pretend you are okay for anyone, including Me. I am not asking you to fix your grief before coming to Me. Bring it as it is, raw and honest. I can hold it.

I am with you in the waiting, in the questions that have no answers yet. I am with you when tears come without warning and when silence feels heavier than words. I am gentle with your heart, and I will continue to be.

One day, this pain will not define every breath you take. Healing will come, slowly and tenderly, in ways that honor what you lost rather than erase it. Until then, rest here. You are not alone. I am holding you, even now.

Day 27
Grief Is Love That Remains

Matthew 5:4

Blessed are those who mourn, for they will be comforted.

Psalm 147:3

He heals the brokenhearted and binds up their wounds.

My precious daughter,

I see your grief. I see the ache that settles deep in your heart and the quiet moments when the weight of loss feels too heavy to carry.

Nothing about your sorrow is hidden from Me. I am close to you now, even closer than you realize.

Grief is not a sign of weak faith. It is love that has nowhere to go. It is the evidence of connection, of meaning, of someone or something that mattered deeply.

You do not need to rush through this pain or pretend that it does not hurt.

Come to Me honestly.

Loss has not changed who you are or how I see you. I hold your memories, your longing, and your unanswered questions with great care.

Healing does not mean forgetting. It means allowing Me to meet you in the grief and slowly restore what has been wounded.

This is a journey, and you are allowed to take it one step at a time.

Bring Me your tears. Speak the truth of your pain. I am patient with your sorrow.

My child, you are deeply loved. Let Me carry what feels too heavy.

Day 28
When Sorrow Leads You Closer to Me

2 Corinthians 7:10

Godly sorrow brings repentance that leads to salvation and leaves no regret, but worldly sorrow brings death.

My precious daughter,

I do not delight in your pain, but I rejoice in what I am bringing forth from it. What you have walked through has not been wasted.

Your sorrow has led you closer to Me.

There was a time of grieving, and it was real. I saw the pain you carried and the weight that rested on your heart. But even there, I was drawing you deeper, softening your heart and leading you into a stronger relationship with Me.

This is not the end of your story.

This is transformation.

Let go of the sorrow that keeps you looking backward and holding onto what cannot be changed.

What you have walked through does not define what is ahead.

I am bringing you into newness.

Lift your eyes.

Release what is behind you.

Step forward into what is before you.

You are not defined by what you have lost.

You are being shaped for what is eternal.

Come forward with Me.

Day 29
When You Begin to Feel Light Again

Isaiah 60:1

Arise, shine, for your light has come, and the glory of the Lord rises upon you.

Psalm 18:28

You, Lord, keep my lamp burning; my God turns my darkness into light.

My precious daughter,

When light begins to return after a long season of darkness, it can bring more than relief.

There can be joy.

There can be wonder.

And sometimes, there is even fear.

After walking through deep pain, your heart learns to be cautious. Part of you welcomes the light, and another part hesitates, unsure if it will last.

This is part of healing. You do not have to rush past it.

And as the weight begins to lift, you may wonder what that means for the love you carried through your suffering.

Let this settle gently in your heart:

Your love does not diminish even as your suffering does.

You are not losing anything by healing. You are being restored.

Stay with Me in this transition.

Let yourself receive the light again, little by little.

You are safe here.

My precious daughter, I am with you in the darkness, and I am with you in the light.

Day 30
Joy After the Night

Psalm 30:5

Weeping may stay for the night, but rejoicing comes in the morning.

John 16:20

You will grieve, but your grief will turn to joy.

My precious daughter,

There was a night when weeping stayed with you, when sorrow felt close, and rest felt distant. I did not rush you through that night. I stayed with you in it. Your tears were not wasted, and your grief was not a weakness. It was love expressing itself honestly.

There is a time to weep and a time to laugh, a time to mourn and a time to dance. These seasons are not in conflict with one another. Laughter does not erase what you have lost, and joy does not cancel the depth of your love. They can live together in your heart without betraying one another.

When joy begins to return, let it come. Let it arrive softly, without explanation or apology. You are not forgetting. You are healing. You are not moving past your story. You are carrying it with more tenderness and strength.

I am exchanging ashes for beauty in ways that honor what was burned and what remains. I am pouring joy where mourning once settled, not to deny the pain, but to remind you that life still flows through you. This is not the end of your story.

Morning comes, sometimes slowly, sometimes quietly. When it does, receive it. I am with you in the night, and I am with you in the joy that follows. Your heart is allowed to live again, and I am holding you through it all.

Rise and Step Forward

Revelation 21:4–5

He will wipe every tear from their eyes. There will be no more death or mourning or crying or pain, for the old order of things has passed away. He who was seated on the throne said, I am making everything new! Then he said, Write this down, for these words are trustworthy and true.

My precious daughter,

Let Me comfort you.

Come close and allow Me to meet you here. I see your tears and the heaviness you have been carrying.

Nothing about your pain has been hidden from Me.

You do not have to hold everything together in your own strength. You can release what you have been carrying and let Me hold you in it.

There has been a time for grieving, and I have been with you through all of it.

But now, I am calling you forward.

It is time to rise.

The past does not have the authority to keep you bound.

What has been lost or broken does not define your future.

I am bringing you into healing, restoration, and new life.

This does not mean you forget what has been. It means you are no longer being held captive by it.

Take My hand.

You are not being left behind in your pain.

You are being led forward. Walk with Me into what is new.

Day 32
When You Forget Yourself

Mark 12:31

Love your neighbor as yourself. There is no commandment greater than these.

Psalm 139:14

I praise you because I am fearfully and wonderfully made; your works are wonderful, I know that full well.

My precious daughter,

I see how often you place yourself last, trying to keep peace and become what others need, even when it leaves your own heart weary and unseen.

And slowly, without realizing it, you begin to lose sight of who you are.

Your joy feels distant. Your peace feels fragile. Your heart grows tired from always pouring out and rarely receiving.

But listen gently to what is true.

I did not create you to disappear beneath the expectations of others. Your life carries value because you are Mine. Your heart matters to Me.

Love was never meant to require the loss of yourself.

Even Jesus stepped away to rest. He loved deeply, yet remained rooted in truth and peace. I am calling you to live that way too.

Come back to Me.

Back to the truth of who you are in Me. Back to the steadiness of My love. Back to the peace that comes from remaining close to Me.

You do not need to shrink yourself to be loved.

Remain close to Me, and I will teach you how to love others without losing the heart I created within you. My precious child, you are deeply loved, fully seen, and safely held by Me.

Day 33
Still Standing Because I Held You

Psalm 28:7

*The Lord is my strength and my shield; my heart trusts in him,
and he helps me.*

2 Corinthians 4:8–9

*We are hard pressed on every side, but not crushed; perplexed, but
not in despair; persecuted, but not abandoned; struck down, but
not destroyed.*

My precious daughter,

I am your strength and your shield. You are stronger than you realize, not because life has been easy, but because you have endured what could have defeated you. Through every battle, I have never left you.

You have walked through moments you never thought you could face. There were days when you felt like giving up, when the weight felt too much, and when you wondered how you would keep going. Yet here you are, still standing, not because you carried yourself, but because I carried you.

You have wiped your tears in moments no one else saw. You carried pain quietly, gathered yourself, and kept moving forward. I saw every tear and knew every ache. Nothing you endured was hidden from Me, and nothing you walked through was faced alone.

When you felt weak, I was your strength. When your steps felt unsteady, I upheld you. Even when you could not feel Me, I was there, sustaining you in ways you could not see.

What was meant to break you has drawn you closer to Me. Through hardship, your trust has deepened, and our relationship has grown. You did not turn away. Even when it was hard, you came back to Me again and again.

You are not standing today by accident. You are standing because I am with you, and I always will be. The same strength that carried you through will continue to sustain you.

Rest in this truth. You are still standing because I held you.

Healing Happens Slowly

Colossians 3:10

and have put on the new self, which is being renewed in knowledge in the image of its Creator.

1 John 3:2

Dear friends, now we are children of God, and what we will be has not yet been made known. But we know that when Christ appears, we shall be like him, for we shall see him as he is.

My precious daughter,

Healing is rarely sudden.

Most often, it unfolds quietly, little by little, in ways you do not always notice at first.

There are moments when you may feel frustrated that you are not farther along, moments when you wonder why the ache has not disappeared completely or why parts of your heart still feel unfinished.

But this does not mean healing is absent.

Transformation takes place in stages.

And even now, something within you is changing. What once felt completely lifeless is beginning to soften. What once felt heavy all the time is beginning to breathe again.

You may not yet feel fully restored, but you are no longer where you once were.

Do not become discouraged by the space between who you were and who you are becoming.

I am present in that space too.

I am not only the author of beginnings.

I am also faithful in the slow work of restoration.

My precious child, be patient with yourself.

What is unfolding within you is becoming whole again.

Day 35
Bring Me Your Frustration

Psalm 62:8

Trust in him at all times, you people; pour out your hearts to him, for God is our refuge.

Psalm 13:1–2

How long, Lord? Will you forget me forever? How long will you hide your face from me? How long must I wrestle with my thoughts and day after day have sorrow in my heart?

My precious daughter,

I know there are moments when you feel angry with Me. I know there are questions you are afraid to ask, disappointments you have tried to bury, and prayers that felt unanswered or misunderstood. You do not have to hide this from Me. I already know what is in your heart, and I am not offended by your honesty.

Your anger does not separate you from Me. It does not shock Me or make you unfaithful. It tells Me that you cared deeply, that you hoped boldly, and that you trusted enough to feel the pain when things did not unfold as you expected. I would rather you bring Me your anger than carry it alone.

You do not need to protect Me from your emotions. My love for you is not threatened by your questions. When you feel confused, disappointed, or even hurt by Me, come closer, not farther away. I can hold your frustration just as I hold your grief.

There are things you may not understand yet, and losses that still ache without explanation. I am not asking you to pretend those things do not hurt. I am asking you to stay with Me in the tension, to let Me sit with you until trust can breathe again.

I am patient with your process. I am gentle with your heart. Even when you are angry, I am still for you. Even when your faith feels strained, I am still holding you. Nothing you feel disqualifies you from My presence.

Bring Me your anger. Bring Me your questions. Bring Me your disappointment. I am here, and I am not leaving.

Day 36
The Years Were Not Wasted

Joel 2:25–26

I will repay you for the years the locusts have eaten… You will have plenty to eat, until you are full, and you will praise the name of the Lord your God.

Psalm 56:8

Record my misery; list my tears on your scroll, are they not in your record?

My precious daughter,

I see the moments when silence feels heavy, and the past seems louder than hope for the future. I know the questions that rise in your heart, wondering where the years went, how life became so painful, or whether too much has been lost to ever be restored.

I know the ache of feeling misunderstood, unheard, or forgotten. I see the weight of regrets you still carry, and the quiet sorrow over things you wish had been different.

But My child, the years that feel wasted are not the end of your story. I am a restorer and a redeemer. I bring beauty from ashes and healing from brokenness. Nothing in your life is beyond My reach, and nothing has changed My love for you.

I do not define you by the mistakes you made, the paths that wounded you, or the moments when you lost your way. I see your heart, and I see the ways you have longed for peace, healing, and understanding.

Not one tear has gone unnoticed by Me. I have seen the heartbreak you carried quietly, the nights when sleep would not come, and the moments when you felt alone. I have been near through all of it, watching over you with compassion and tenderness.

You are not disqualified from My love or My promises.

Come to Me now. You do not have to carry shame or fear any longer. Let Me fill your heart with My peace and guide you gently forward. I will lead you one step at a time, restoring what feels broken and strengthening what has grown weary. Your story is not over, My precious child. I am still writing it with hope, purpose, and redemption.

When You Do Not Understand

Isaiah 55:8–9

For my thoughts are not your thoughts, neither are your ways my ways, declares the Lord. As the heavens are higher than the earth, so are my ways higher than your ways and my thoughts than your thoughts.

Proverbs 3:5–6

Trust in the Lord with all your heart and lean not on your own understanding; in all your ways submit to him, and he will make your paths straight.

My precious daughter,

I know how hard it is to follow Me when nothing seems to make sense. I see the confusion you carry, the questions that remain unanswered, and the quiet ache that comes when the pain feels unnecessary or unfair. There are days when the process feels heavier than you imagined you could bear, and I want you to know that I see all of it.

I am not distant from your struggle. I am not overlooking your tears or minimizing how difficult this feels. I understand the disappointment of waiting, the exhaustion of trusting without clarity, and the loneliness that can settle in when relief does not come quickly. Your weariness matters to Me.

Even here, when understanding feels out of reach, I gently ask you to keep walking with Me. Not because you have everything figured out, but because you are not meant to carry this alone. My love for you has never wavered. It has not weakened in your questions, and it has not withdrawn in your pain.

My ways are higher than your ways, and My thoughts higher than your thoughts, but that does not mean I am careless with your heart. There will come a time when you look back and recognize how I was protecting you in ways you could not see, guiding you, even when the path felt uncertain. I was with you then, and I am with you now.

You do not need to rush your trust or force your faith. Just stay close. Let Me hold you through what you do not understand. I know what I am doing, and I am doing it with love, patience, and care for you. Trust Me. You are safe with Me.

Day 38
Resting in the Waiting

Psalm 46:10

Be still, and know that I am God.

Psalm 62:5–6

Yes, my soul, find rest in God; my hope comes from him.

My precious daughter,

I know this season feels tiring. I know there are moments when resting feels difficult because your heart wants answers, movement, or relief. It is hard to sit still when you are unsure how long this will last or what comes next. I see that tension within you, and I am not disappointed by it.

Rest here, even when it feels uncomfortable. You do not need to push yourself to understand or resolve everything right now. This season is not asking you to strive. It is asking you to breathe, to soften, and to let yourself be held.

Rest in My sovereignty. I know it can be hard to trust when things do not look the way you hoped. When expectations go unmet, disappointment can quietly settle in your heart. I am aware of that weight, and I am steady, even when life feels uncertain.

Release the expectations that are pressing on you, not because they were wrong, but because they are heavy. You do not have to carry timelines, outcomes, or comparisons that exhaust you. I am inviting you to let Me hold what you were never meant to manage alone.

Respond with patience, especially toward yourself. You are not failing because you feel weary or unsure. Patience is not something you must manufacture. It grows as you remain close to Me.

You are not behind. You are not wasting time. This season is not empty. I am with you here, tending to your heart, working quietly beneath the surface, and caring for you with intention and love. Rest, My child. You are safe in My care.

Day 39
When You Try to Control Everything

Matthew 10:29–31

Are not two sparrows sold for a penny? Yet not one of them will fall to the ground outside your Father's care. And even the very hairs of your head are all numbered. So don't be afraid; you are worth more than many sparrows.

James 4:14–15

Why, you do not even know what will happen tomorrow. What is your life? You are a mist that appears for a little while and then vanishes. Instead, you ought to say, If it is the Lord's will, we will live and do this or that.

My precious daughter,

I see how carefully you move through your days.

How you try to protect yourself from being hurt.

How you weigh your decisions, watching for what could go wrong, trying to make sure everything is just right.

I see the effort behind that. I know you are trying to stay safe.

But listen gently to Me.

You do not have to carry that much control.

Not every step needs to be perfect.

Not every choice needs to protect you from every possible pain.

Most things are not as fragile as they feel.

And most mistakes are not the end.

They are part of learning. Part of growing.

You do not have to plan your life so tightly that there is no room to breathe.

There is space to explore. There is space to try.

I am with you in all of it.

Not just when you get it right, but in every step.

I did not create you to live imprisoned by fear, but to walk closely with Me in trust.

My child, stay close to Me and listen to Me. I will guide you.

The Courage to Risk

Joshua 1:9

Have I not commanded you? Be strong and courageous. Do not be afraid; do not be discouraged, for the Lord your God will be with you wherever you go.

2 Timothy 1:7

For the Spirit God gave us does not make us timid, but gives us power, love and self-discipline.

My precious daughter,

I see the hesitation in your heart.

There is a part of you that wants to move forward. And a part of you that has learned, through hard experience, that moving forward can hurt.

I understand that.

But a guarded life can only grow so far.

Loving people will sometimes bring disappointment. Honesty can create discomfort. And to become who you are meant to be will always require courage.

This is part of living. And I am with you in all of it.

You do not have to wait until there is no risk. You do not have to be certain before you move. You only need to trust that I am with you in every step, whether it leads to what you hoped for or something different.

You are not defined by the outcome. You are shaped by the courage to step forward.

I know you have been brave before and walked away wounded. I am not asking you to forget that. I am asking you to trust Me anyway.

Stay close to Me.

My precious child, you are safe with Me, even when life feels uncertain.

Day 41
One Step at a Time

Psalm 32:8

I will instruct you and teach you in the way you should go, I will counsel you with my loving eye on you.

Psalm 119:105

Your word is a lamp to my feet and a light to my path.

My precious daughter,

I know you wonder about the future. I see the questions that rise in your heart and the desire to understand what lies ahead. And I also see something beneath those questions — a weariness that comes from not knowing. From waiting for clarity that has not yet come. From taking steps you were not sure about, and still not being able to see very far ahead.

But the future is not for you to carry all at once. I will reveal it as it is needed, in the right time and in the right measure. Not because I am withholding from you, but because I am protecting you. The full picture, seen all at once, would overwhelm what I am carefully building within you.

I give light for today so that you remain close to Me, moving in trust, obedience, and safety rather than fear or control.

This is how I protect you. This is how I guide you. Staying dependent on Me keeps your heart aligned and your steps steady. You are never walking blindly, even when the path feels quiet.

I know it can be hard to live this way. To release the need to see further than I am showing you. But as you learn to take one step at a time, something begins to shift. The anxiety of the unknown loses its grip. Peace begins to replace the need for answers.

Walk forward with peace. Take the step before you, not the one far ahead. I am with you now, and I will be with you as each new step is revealed. You are secure in Me, My precious child. You do not have to see it all to be safe.

My Grace Is Enough

2 Corinthians 12:9

But he said to me, My grace is sufficient for you, for my power is made perfect in weakness.

My precious daughter,

I know how heavy things have felt for you. I see the places where you feel worn down, uncertain, and quietly discouraged. I know the moments when your weakness feels exposed, and your prayers feel unanswered. Hear this gently and clearly: My grace is sufficient for you, and My power is revealed most clearly when you feel you have none left.

I am bigger than your hurt, your mistakes, your shame, your worry, your past, your regrets, your pain, your doubts, and your fears. None of these surprise Me or push Me away.

Right now, My child, I want you to know this. What you have been praying about has not been ignored. I am arranging things with care, even when it feels slow or invisible. Waiting can be painful, especially when you are already tired, but you are not forgotten. Have faith, even when it is not easy. Trust Me, one step at a time.

Do not judge your life by what you have seen so far or by what you have endured. Pain does not tell the whole story. Your past does not cancel your future. What feels unfinished is still being formed in My hands.

You are never forgotten. You are never rejected. You have always been Mine, even on the days you felt far away or unsure. I am with you in the waiting, in the weakness, and in the hope you are still learning to hold.

Rest here for a moment. Breathe. My grace is enough for you, and I am not going anywhere.

Day 43
Do Not Be Afraid, Trust Me

Isaiah 41:10

So do not fear, for I am with you; do not be dismayed, for I am your God. I will strengthen you and help you; I will uphold you with my righteous right hand.

Psalm 37:5

Commit your way to the Lord; trust in him and he will act.

My beloved daughter,

Do not be afraid. I see the thoughts that trouble your heart, how your mind races ahead trying to prepare for what feels uncertain. Bring those thoughts to Me. You were never meant to carry them alone.

I know how real and convincing fear can be, but it does not hold your future. I do.

Trust Me, even when you do not understand the way forward. I am already working in what you cannot see. There is nothing ahead of you that is beyond My care.

When fear tells you that you are not strong enough, remember that My strength is made perfect in your weakness. When it tells you the future is unsafe, remember that I am already there, preparing the way before you.

Let go of the need to figure everything out or control what has not yet come. As you trust Me step by step, I will steady your path and guide you with My peace.

I am with you. I will help you. I will uphold you. You are held.

Be still and let your heart rest in Me instead of fear. You do not need to see the whole path to take the next step. I am holding you, and I will not let you fall.

Day 44
Safe in My Hands

Psalm 121:5–6

The Lord watches over you, the Lord is your shade at your right hand; the sun will not harm you by day, nor the moon by night.

1 Peter 5:7

Cast all your anxiety on him because he cares for you.

My precious daughter,

Tell Me what you are afraid of. Speak it honestly. You never have to hide your fears from Me or carry them alone. I see what worries you in the quiet moments, the thoughts that return when everything is still, and the concerns you try to manage on your own. Nothing you face is beyond My knowledge or My power, and I am not overwhelmed by what feels overwhelming to you. I am present, steady, and fully able to care for you.

You do not need to be afraid to ask Me anything. Come to Me with openness and trust. I hold the world in the palm of My hand, and the same hands that formed the heavens are holding you even now. Nothing can slip through My fingers. You are not exposed. You are not unprotected.

When fear tries to rise, do not pull away from Me. Come closer. Sit with Me and let your heart rest. You do not need to brace yourself or prepare for the worst. I delight in caring for you, in covering you with peace, and in reminding you that you are held in a love that does not change. As your Father, I watch over your life with tenderness and strength.

Even the things you do not understand are not outside of My care. Even the situations that feel uncertain are not beyond My reach. I am already present in what is ahead of you, just as I am with you now. You are safe to trust Me.

As you remain with Me, fear will begin to loosen its hold. Your breath will steady. Your thoughts will quiet. I will guard your heart and guide your steps. I will go before you and stand behind you. You are not facing anything alone.

Day 45
Let Me Carry What You Were Never Meant to Hold

Matthew 11:28–30

Come to me, all you who are weary and burdened, and I will give you rest… For my yoke is easy and my burden is light.

1 Peter 5:7

Cast all your anxiety on him because he cares for you.

My precious daughter,

I see how much you have been carrying, the weight of your responsibilities, the pressure you place on yourself, and the quiet fear about what lies ahead. Even small things begin to feel heavy when you try to hold them all on your own.

Tell Me honestly, are you resting? Are you allowing your body and mind to be restored, or are you pushing forward, trying to manage everything without pause? I see how your thoughts run ahead, trying to prepare for what has not yet come, and I know how easily fear of the future can settle into your heart.

You were never meant to carry all of this alone.

Walk with Me. Bring Me what feels too heavy. Give Me the burdens you keep trying to manage, the pressure to hold everything together, and the thoughts that will not quiet. I am not asking you to carry more. I am asking you to release what was never yours to hold.

My burden is light, not because life has no weight, but because I carry it with you. When you place these things in My hands, you are trusting Me with them. As you do, the pressure begins to lift, and anxiety begins to loosen its hold on your heart.

You do not need to force peace or control every outcome. Let Me care for you. Let Me teach you a better way, one that is steady, restful, and rooted in trust.

Stay close to Me. Walk with Me step by step. You are not behind, and you are not alone. I am carrying what concerns you, and I will lead you gently forward.

Let Go So Your Heart Can Live Free

Ephesians 4:31–32

Get rid of all bitterness, rage, and anger… Be kind and compassionate to one another, forgiving each other, just as in Christ God forgave you.

Matthew 6:14

For if you forgive other people when they sin against you, your heavenly Father will also forgive you.

My precious daughter,

I see the places where you are still holding tightly to what has hurt you, the words that linger, the disappointments that wounded you, and the ways others have failed you. I understand why you have held on. It felt like protection. Like control. Like a way to keep your heart from being hurt again.

But what you are holding is also holding you.

I know it is not easy to let go. Part of you fears that releasing it means what happened did not matter, or that you will be left unprotected. But holding on has been costing you more than you realize.

These wounds begin to shape the way you see everything. They create distance where you long for closeness and build walls where your heart is actually yearning for connection. You were not created to live guarded in this way.

Unforgiveness does not only keep others at a distance, it also isolates you. It fills your heart with heaviness, mistrust, and fear that I never intended for you to carry.

I am not asking you to pretend the pain was small. I am asking you to release it into My hands. Forgiveness is not saying what happened was acceptable. It is choosing freedom instead of continuing to carry what is hurting you.

Come to Me with what still aches inside you. Let Me help you loosen your grip gently and patiently. You do not have to force healing or do this all at once. Stay close to Me, and I will lead your heart into freedom.

You are not meant to live guarded. You are meant to live free.

Day 47
There Will Come a Day

Psalm 30:11

You turned my wailing into dancing; you removed my sackcloth and clothed me with joy.

Isaiah 43:18–19

Forget the former things... See, I am doing a new thing!

My precious daughter,

There will come a day when the weight you once carried no longer defines you. The places that once felt broken within you will begin to heal, and even those who knew your pain will see the difference.

Not because of your own strength, but because of My mercy and My love at work within you.

I know there are days when healing still feels far away, when you wonder if your heart will ever feel light again. But you are not simply surviving anymore. I am leading you into wholeness, restoration, and new life.

At first, the change may feel small and quiet. You may only notice little moments, a lighter heart, a deeper peace, the return of hope where there was once only heaviness. But slowly, you will begin to see what I have been doing within you all along.

Wonder will begin to rise again.

Hope will begin to awaken again.

And the future will no longer feel so far away.

My child, your restoration is beginning. Do not stay bound to what is behind you. Walk forward with Me and trust what I am growing in your life.

I am turning your mourning into dancing, your sorrow into joy, and your broken places into something beautiful again.

Day 48
Creation Speaks of Me

Psalm 19:1

The heavens declare the glory of God; the skies proclaim the work of his hands.

Romans 1:20

For since the creation of the world God's invisible qualities have been clearly seen, being understood from what has been made.

My precious daughter,

When pain has stayed with you for a long time, something quietly
shifts. You stop noticing. The flowers bloom and you do not see them.
The light changes in the evening sky and you walk past it. Beauty is still
there, but grief has a way of narrowing your world until only the ache is
visible.

So when you begin to notice again, pay attention. That is not a small
thing.

When you stop long enough to stand in awe of the mountains, listen to
the power of the ocean, or bend down to smell a flower, something
within you is waking up. You are drawing close to Me, and I am
drawing close to you.

This world was created by My hands, and you are part of that creation.
You were made to live within this rhythm of beauty, wonder, and
peace. Your soul remembers where it came from. Creation speaks of
Me.

There is a quiet connection that happens when you walk through a
field, sit beneath a tree, or stand silently in a forest. Something settles.
The noise within you begins to quiet. Your breath slows. That is not
accidental. I designed this world not only to sustain you, but to draw
you back to yourself and back to Me.

Noticing beauty again is a sign that healing is happening. It means your
heart is beginning to open after a long season of protecting itself. Do
not rush past these moments. Let them be what they are, gentle
evidence that you are coming back to life.

Slow down. Notice what is around you. Let gratitude rise where
heaviness once lived. My child, I am present in these quiet moments.
And so, slowly, are you.

Guarding Your Heart From Bitterness

Hebrews 12:15

See to it that no one falls short of the grace of God and that no bitter root grows up to cause trouble and defile many.

Colossians 3:13

Bear with each other and forgive one another if any of you has a grievance against someone. Forgive as the Lord forgave you.

My precious daughter,

I see how disappointment can linger when something has hurt you deeply. What began as pain can slowly turn into something heavier. Thoughts begin to replay, wrongs begin to collect, and without realizing it, your heart starts to close.

This is how bitterness takes root.

It may begin with what was done to you, but if it remains, it will begin shaping how you see yourself, how you feel, and how you move through your days.

I do not want that for you.

You were not created to carry this weight. You are free to release it.

You do not have to keep holding on to what continues to wound you. Let it go gently, step by step.

Forgiveness is not pretending it did not matter. It is choosing not to let it take more from you.

As you release what has hurt you, your heart begins to open again. Joy returns. Peace settles. Life feels lighter.

Stay close to Me in this. I will help you let go of what you were never meant to carry.

You are not meant to live hardened. You are meant to live free.

Day 50
I See What Has Been Done

Romans 12:19

Do not take revenge, my dear friends, but leave room for God's wrath, for it is written: 'It is mine to avenge; I will repay,' says the Lord.

Psalm 34:18

The Lord is close to the brokenhearted and saves those who are crushed in spirit.

My precious daughter,

I see what has been done to you.

I see the words that were spoken, the moments that hurt, and the ways others have treated you unfairly. Nothing has been hidden from Me. Nothing has gone unnoticed.

I know how it still lingers, stirring old pain and wounds you try to quiet. I see the weight it carries in your heart.

But you do not need to fight this battle.

You do not have to defend yourself or carry the burden of making it right. I am your defender. I see clearly, and you can trust Me with what is beyond your control.

Trust Me with what was done to you.

When you release it into My hands, you are not saying it did not matter. You are trusting Me to bring justice in My way and in My time.

You do not have to wait for them to understand or admit what they did. I will vindicate you.

When you release what you cannot control, your heart begins to breathe again. Space opens where heaviness once lived.

You are safe to let it go.

My precious child, trust Me with what has hurt you, and let your heart rest in My care.

Day 51
Love Is Not Your Weakness

1 Corinthians 13:4–7

Love is patient, love is kind. It does not envy, it does not boast, it is not proud. It does not dishonor others, it is not self-seeking, it is not easily angered, it keeps no record of wrongs. Love does not delight in evil but rejoices with the truth. It always protects, always trusts, always hopes, always perseveres.

Proverbs 4:23

Above all else, guard your heart, for everything you do flows from it.

My precious daughter,

Your love, your beautiful heart, is not what caused the betrayal. What was done to you came from what was broken in them, not from what was good in you.

Do not make yourself the problem.

I see how you have tried to protect yourself. How you have wondered if you should be less open, less trusting, less loving, just so you would not be hurt again.

But do not hide what is beautiful in you.

Do not harden your heart in response to what was done. Do not close yourself off or punish yourself for someone else's inability to see your worth. Their actions came from their own pain, not from your lack of value.

Your love is not a flaw.

Love is patient.

Love is kind.

Love heals, restores, and brings life.

And that is what I placed inside of you.

You are not wrong for loving deeply. You are not weak for caring. What is in you is good, and it reflects My heart.

Do not be afraid of love.

Let Me teach you how to love with wisdom, without losing the beauty of who you are.

My precious child, your heart is still good.

Day 52
Trust the Detour

Isaiah 30:21

Whether you turn to the right or to the left, your ears will hear a voice behind you, saying, This is the way; walk in it.

James 1:2–4

Consider it pure joy whenever you face trials of many kinds, because you know that the testing of your faith produces perseverance.

My precious daughter,

I know how unsettling it feels when plans suddenly change, and life unfolds differently than you expected. I see the disappointment and confusion that rise when what once felt certain becomes unclear. There are moments when you wonder why doors close, why delays happen, or why things seem to unravel despite your prayers and effort. I know those moments have been difficult for you.

Do not be afraid when life takes an unexpected turn. Not every disruption is a setback, and not every detour is a mistake. Even when things appear to be falling apart, I am still at work. What feels confusing to you is not confusing to Me.

Learn to trust Me when things do not go according to your plans. What feels like an interruption may actually be protection. What seems like rejection may be redirection. What appears to be delay may be preparation for something you cannot yet see.

Stay close to Me when questions rise and your heart feels weary. Lean on My strength when yours feels small. Rest in My love when understanding feels out of reach. I am guiding you with patience and care, even when you cannot yet see the full picture.

Walk with trust rather than fear. My love for you has never wavered, and My presence has never left you. Even in the detours, I am faithfully leading you forward.

My precious child, you are never walking alone.

Day 53
It Is Not Too Late to Run Your Race

Hebrews 12:1–2

Therefore, since we are surrounded by such a great cloud of witnesses, let us throw off everything that hinders and the sin that so easily entangles. And let us run with perseverance the race marked out for us, fixing our eyes on Jesus, the pioneer and perfecter of faith. For the joy set before him he endured the cross, scorning its shame, and sat down at the right hand of the throne of God.

My precious daughter,

I see you watching from the edges of your own life. Waiting for the right moment. Waiting until you feel ready. Waiting until the fear subsides or the path becomes clearer. I understand why you have stayed there. The sidelines felt safer than the risk of stepping forward again.

But I am calling you off the sidelines now.

It is not too late. Not for you. Not for what I have placed within you. Not for the life I have been preparing you for through everything you have walked through. What you have survived has not disqualified you. It has been forming you.

Let go of what was, and allow yourself to begin receiving what can be. You have carried disappointment, fear, and the quiet grief of missed opportunities long enough. I am not asking you to pretend those things did not happen. I am asking you to stop letting them have the final word over your future.

Prepare your heart to receive what I have for you. Align your thoughts and your steps with Me. As you surrender your fears and your need for control, you will begin to recognize My hand moving in ways you could not see before. What once felt heavy will begin to lift. What once felt impossible will begin to open before you.

You do not need to feel fully ready before you move. Faith often requires movement before certainty. You only need the willingness to rise, to trust Me, and to walk forward with expectation.

Take the next step, My precious daughter. I will meet you there.

Day 54
You Are Unfolding

Romans 5:3–4

We also glory in our sufferings, because we know that suffering produces perseverance; perseverance, character; and character, hope.

Galatians 6:9

Let us not become weary in doing good, for at the proper time we will reap a harvest if we do not give up.

My precious daughter,

When a seed is planted in the ground, it does not grow without pressure. It pushes through the soil, stretching and rising in ways that are not always comfortable.

There are moments when it feels like you are bending, like you might break under the weight of what you are carrying. There are places that still ache, places you were afraid would never stop hurting. I see them.

But you are not stuck. You are unfolding.

Every day you choose to keep going, even when it is hard, is proof that something is changing within you. You are becoming who you were created to be.

Healing takes time, especially the deeper places. Let Me work there. Let Me restore what has been wounded, even when it feels slow.

What feels like pain now will not always feel this way. One day, what once hurt will no longer define you.

It will become strength.

It will deepen your compassion. It will allow you to love in ways you could not before, because you have walked through what others are still facing.

Nothing you have gone through has been wasted.

You are not meant to stay in this pain. You are moving through it, step by step, with Me.

My precious child, you are growing, even now.

A Future Held in Hope

Jeremiah 29:11

For I know the plans I have for you, declares the Lord, plans to prosper you and not to harm you, plans to give you hope and a future.

Jeremiah 33:3

Call to me, and I will answer you and tell you great and unsearchable things you do not know.

My precious daughter,

I know that sometimes hearing about hope feels difficult when you are tired, discouraged, or unsure of what comes next. I see the questions you carry and the weight that settles in your heart when the future feels unclear. You are not wrong for feeling this way, and you are not failing Me.

Still, I want you to know this: I know the plans I have for you. They are not plans to harm you or hurt you, even when the path has included pain. My intentions toward you have always been shaped by love. I am holding a future for you that carries hope, even if you cannot see it yet.

You do not need to have everything figured out. You do not need to force understanding or rush ahead. Come to Me just as you are, with your doubts, your fears, and your longing for reassurance. I am gentle with you.

As you draw near, I will show you what you need to know, one step at a time. I will reveal great and mighty things in ways you can receive, at a pace your heart can bear. I will guide you with patience and care.

My child, rest in this truth: you are not forgotten, you are not delayed beyond purpose, and you are not alone. I am with you, and My plans for you are still unfolding in hope.

Day 56
Faith Formed in the Fire

Isaiah 43:2

When you pass through the waters, I will be with you; and when you pass through the rivers, they will not sweep over you.

Psalm 66:10

For you, God, tested us; you refined us like silver.

My precious daughter,

I know there are moments when what you are carrying feels exhausting. There are days when the pressure feels constant, when your heart grows weary from trying to stay strong, and when you quietly wonder how much longer you can keep walking through this season. I see the fear, the discouragement, and the questions you carry beneath the surface. You do not have to hide them from Me.

Even here, you are not alone.

I have not stepped away from you in your hardship, and I have not abandoned you in your struggle. When your strength feels small, I remain steady. When fear tries to rise, My presence is still surrounding you. Even when you cannot see how I am working, I am near, attentive, and faithful through every moment.

What you are walking through is not meant to destroy you. I am carefully refining you like silver, strengthening what is precious within you and shaping your faith with tenderness and purpose. This season is developing endurance, wisdom, and deeper trust in Me. Though the process feels difficult, it is not without meaning.

Do not let fear take root in your heart. Trust that I am leading you, even when the way forward feels uncertain. I am forming strength in you that will endure long after this season passes. What I am building within you will carry eternal value.

Lean on My strength when yours feels weary. Rest in My presence when your heart feels overwhelmed. You are secure in My care, My precious child, and I will continue walking with you through every fire you face. You are not abandoned. You are being held, strengthened, and lovingly refined.

Day 57
The Way, the Truth, and the Life

John 14:6

Jesus answered, I am the way and the truth and the life. No one comes to the Father except through me.

Psalm 119:105

Your word is a lamp for my feet, a light on my path.

My precious daughter,

I see the moments when you are not sure which way to turn. When the path that once felt clear has grown quiet, and you are wondering if you have somehow missed Me or moved outside of what I had for you. That disorientation is real, and I do not dismiss it. But I want you to hear this clearly.

I am the Way, the Truth, and the Life. When you feel uncertain about where to go, follow Me. When confusion tries to cloud your mind, rest in My truth. When you feel weary or empty, come to Me and receive life.

You do not have to figure everything out on your own. I am not asking you to know every answer, only to stay close to Me. As you walk with Me, I will guide your steps. As you listen to Me, I will steady your heart. As you trust Me, I will lead you forward with clarity and peace.

There will be moments when the path feels unclear, and your thoughts feel unsettled. In those moments, come back to what you know is true. My truth does not shift with your circumstances or your emotions. It remains firm when everything else feels uncertain. Let My truth quiet the noise around you and within you.

I am your source of life, hope, and peace. When you stay connected to Me, you will not lose your way. Even when the road feels narrow or unfamiliar, it is safe when you walk with Me. You are not navigating this life alone. I am guiding you every step of the way.

My child, walk forward without fear. Stay rooted in truth. Live each day from the peace, purpose, and identity I have given you.

Walk in Love, Not Fear

1 John 4:18

There is no fear in love. But perfect love drives out fear.

Romans 8:15

The Spirit you received does not make you slaves so that you live in fear again; rather, the Spirit you received brought about your adoption to sonship.

My precious daughter,

You were not created to live in constant fear of getting everything wrong.

I see how much energy it takes. The measuring, the second-guessing, the quiet exhaustion of checking and rechecking every step. I see how fear has whispered that if you just think it through one more time, prepare a little more carefully, or hold yourself to a higher standard, you will finally feel safe enough to move forward.

But fear does not deliver what it promises. It takes more than it gives. It has kept you from stepping forward when I was calling you. It has made you hesitate at doors I had already opened. It has cost you rest, joy, and the freedom of simply being loved without having to earn it.

This is what happens when fear becomes your guide. But I did not call you to walk with Me in fear. I called you to walk with Me in love.

When you stay close to Me, you do not have to live trapped in endless striving and anxious self-examination. Love brings trust. Love brings peace. Love allows your heart to rest in the confidence that I am leading you.

There is a rhythm to walking with Me that is steady and secure. You do not have to hold your life together through control and worry. I already hold it in My hands.

As you learn to walk in love instead of fear, your heart will begin to settle. You will stop living as though everything depends entirely on you. And you will begin to experience the peace that comes from trusting the One who is guiding your steps. My child, walk with Me and let My love lead you.

Day 59
Learning to Love Again

1 John 4:18

There is no fear in love. But perfect love drives out fear.

Psalm 34:18

The Lord is close to the brokenhearted and saves those who are crushed in spirit.

My precious daughter,

I see how your heart has been shaped by what you have walked through.

I know the places where love felt painful, where trust was broken, where something within you learned to be cautious.

I have seen it all. And still, I am here, gently drawing near to you.

I am not asking you to ignore what you have experienced. I am not asking you to forget what you have learned.

But I am inviting you into something new.

You are not the same as you once were.

You have grown.

You have learned.

You are more aware, more discerning than before.

You can hold wisdom and still remain open. You can guard your heart and still allow it to be free.

Fear does not have to lead you anymore. Love is not something you were meant to avoid. It is something you were created to give and to receive.

I am patient with you in this. I am not rushing you.

Just stay with Me. And in time, you will find that love does not have to be something you fear.

My precious daughter, your heart was made for love. And I will gently teach you how to trust it again.

Day 60
You Were Never Meant to Stay Hidden

Matthew 5:14–16

You are the light of the world. A town built on a hill cannot be hidden. Neither do people light a lamp and put it under a bowl. Instead they put it on its stand, and it gives light to everyone in the house. In the same way, let your light shine before others, that they may see your good deeds and glorify your Father in heaven.

Ephesians 2:10

You are the light of the world, and created for good works prepared in advance.

My precious daughter,

I see the ways you have learned to make yourself smaller.

Not all at once, and not always by choice. Somewhere along the way, staying quiet felt safer than being misunderstood. Holding back felt easier than offering what was in you and watching it be dismissed. You learned that being seen could mean being hurt, and so you stepped back. You dimmed what I placed within you, not out of rebellion, but out of protection.

I understand why.

But you were never meant to stay hidden.

There were times when others did not recognize your worth, and times when you questioned it yourself. But I never questioned it. I have always seen who you are, not who pain convinced you to become, but who I created you to be.

As you continue to walk with Me, you will begin to see what I see. The way your presence brings light, comfort, and meaning to those around you. The gifts I placed within you were never meant to remain hidden in the background. They were given to be shared.

You do not need to hold back any longer. You do not have to live in fear of being misunderstood or unseen. Let Me lead you forward. Let Me bring what I placed within you into the light as you walk with Me.

You are not here by accident. What I placed inside of you was intentional, and as you trust Me, it will begin to unfold in beautiful ways. Let your life reflect My love.

Let it shine without fear. My precious child, you no longer have to hide.

Day 61
When You Feel Like You Do Not Belong

Psalm 68:6

God sets the lonely in families, he leads out the prisoners with singing; but the rebellious live in a sun-scorched land.

John 15:15

I no longer call you servants, because a servant does not know his master's business. Instead, I have called you friends, for everything that I learned from my Father I have made known to you.

My precious daughter,

I see the ache you carry when you feel alone or like you don't belong.

Not just alone, but the kind of loneliness that sits deeper, when you feel like you are on the outside of life, watching others connect, laugh, and move forward while you remain on the edge, unsure where you belong.

I see how your thoughts begin to turn inward in those moments. Wondering how you are being perceived. Questioning if you said the wrong thing. Feeling like you do not quite fit, no matter how much you try.

And slowly, without even meaning to, you begin to pull back. Not because you do not want connection, but because it feels safer to step away than to risk being misunderstood, overlooked, or hurt again.

I see that cycle. The longing for connection, and the retreat that follows.

You were not created to live unseen. You are not unlikable. You are not too much or not enough.

You are learning how to trust again. And I am with you in that process.

Just begin with small steps. Stay present a little longer than you normally would. Offer a simple kindness without overthinking it.

My precious child, when fear rises and tells you to withdraw, remember I am with you. We will take these steps together. Rest in the security of My love.

Day 62
Love With Boundaries

Proverbs 4:23

Above all else, guard your heart, for everything you do flows from it.

Philippians 4:7

And the peace of God, which transcends all understanding, will guard your hearts and your minds in Christ Jesus.

My precious daughter,

I see the places where you feel stretched too thin. Where your yes has come too quickly, and your no has felt impossible to say. Where you give more than you have, hoping to keep peace, hoping to be enough.

I want you to understand something gently.

Boundaries are not selfish. They are wise, and they are loving.

They are not meant to separate you from others. They are meant to protect what I have placed within you. Your peace matters. Your time, your energy, and your heart are not things to be given away without care.

You do not have to say yes to everything. You do not have to carry what was never yours to hold.

When you honor the limits I am showing you, you are not failing others. You are learning to walk in wisdom.

Come to Me when something feels heavy, when your heart feels uneasy, when you sense you are giving beyond what is right. I will show you where to step forward and where to step back.

You are not called to live exhausted.

You are called to live in peace, wisdom, and wholeness with Me.

My precious child, let Me help you protect that.

Day 63
Rooted Within

Colossians 2:6–7

So then, just as you received Christ Jesus as Lord, continue to live your lives in him, rooted and built up in him, strengthened in the faith as you were taught, and overflowing with thankfulness.

Psalm 62:5–6

Yes, my soul, find rest in God; my hope comes from him. Truly he is my rock and my salvation; he is my fortress, I will not be shaken.

My precious daughter,

I see how you have looked outside of yourself, hoping someone else would show you your worth. Hoping their attention or approval would quiet the questions within you.

I understand that longing.

But when your worth depends on how someone else sees you, your heart becomes unsteady. You begin to shape yourself around their response, slowly moving away from yourself.

That is not where your security is meant to come from.

Your worth was established long before any relationship entered your life. It does not rise or fall based on who notices you, who chooses you, or who stays.

I am the One who defines you. When you stay rooted in Me, you begin to see yourself clearly. Your values grow steady. You no longer feel the need to become what others expect, because you are grounded in truth.

And from that place, something shifts.

You can stand in a room without questioning your place.

You can be alone without feeling abandoned.

You can connect without losing yourself.

When you receive My love fully, you are no longer searching for someone to complete you. You are able to give and receive love without losing who you are.

My precious child, when the time comes for deeper connection, you will not enter it empty. You will enter it whole.

Day 64
Trust *Me in the Waiting*

Psalm 37:7

Be still before the Lord and wait patiently for him.

Revelation 3:7

*What he opens no one can shut, and what he shuts no one can
open.*

My precious daughter,

I know waiting can feel discouraging. When doors remain closed, and answers do not come as quickly as you hoped, it is easy to wonder if you are being forgotten or left behind. But you are not forgotten, and I am not withholding good from you.

There are seasons when doors open quickly, and seasons when they remain closed, not as punishment, but as protection. Even when you do not understand what I am doing, I am still working on your behalf.

Waiting with Me is never wasted time.

In these quiet places, I am strengthening your faith, steadying your heart, and preparing you for what lies ahead. What feels like delay is often My way of guiding you toward what is truly meant for you.

When I close a door, it is because I see what you cannot see. I am leading you away from what would drain you or pull you away from My peace. And when the right door opens, you will not have to force your way through it. I will make the path clear.

When waiting feels heavy, bring your restlessness to Me. You do not have to carry the uncertainty alone. I am near, even in the silence, and I am gently leading you step by step.

Do not be afraid of where you are right now, My child. What I have for you will not pass you by. Trust My timing. Trust My heart. My child, I am opening the way before you.

Day 65
Honoring What I Created

Psalm 139:14

I praise you because I am fearfully and wonderfully made; your works are wonderful, I know that full well.

1 Corinthians 6:19–20

Do you not know that your bodies are temples of the Holy Spirit, who is in you, whom you have received from God? You are not your own; you were bought at a price. Therefore honor God with your bodies.

My precious daughter,

I created you with care and intention. You are fearfully and wonderfully made, and nothing about you was overlooked. I formed you with love, purpose, and tenderness.

I see the moments when your eyes drift toward others, and you begin to question your own beauty, your worth, or whether you are enough.

That is not the truth of who you are.

I know the relationship you have had with your own body has not always been peaceful. I know there are wounds there that go deeper than comparison alone. I see the harsh thoughts, the insecurity, and the quiet ways you have struggled to see yourself with kindness.

But My child, I have never looked at you with shame.

What you see around you is often shaped, altered, and filtered through unrealistic expectations. But you were never created to reflect an image. You were created to carry something far deeper, My presence, My love, and the beauty of a heart rooted in Me.

Your body is not something to fight against or diminish. It is part of the life I lovingly created for you. Treat it with care, not out of pressure or striving, but out of honor for what I made.

You do not need to change yourself to be worthy.

You are already Mine.

Let your heart rest in that truth, My precious child.

Day 66
Pray My Word and Watch Me Move

Matthew 19:26

With man, this is impossible, but with God, all things are possible.

Isaiah 55:11

So is my word that goes out from my mouth: It will not return to me empty, but will accomplish what I desire.

My precious daughter,

I know there have been moments when prayer felt like speaking into silence. When you brought your heart to Me faithfully, day after day, and the answers did not come the way you hoped. When you wondered if your words were reaching Me at all, or if something about the way you were praying was simply not enough.

I want you to know that none of those prayers were lost. Not one of them.

But I also want to invite you into something deeper. Not a formula or a method, but a way of praying that roots your words in Mine. When you quiet your heart, seek My presence, and pray My Word over your home, your mind, and your future, something begins to shift in ways you may not immediately see.

When you align your voice with My truth, you come into agreement with what I am already doing. My Word carries power. As you speak it in faith, peace begins to replace confusion, hope rises where fear once lived, and clarity starts to form where there was once only uncertainty.

What once felt impossible starts to open. Doors you could not force begin to move. Strength comes where you felt weak. I respond to hearts that seek Me and to words that agree with My truth. Nothing spoken in faith is wasted, even when the answer is still forming beyond what you can see.

Continue to meet with Me. Continue to pray My Word. Let it shape your thoughts, guard your heart, and guide your steps. As you stay aligned with Me, you will begin to see how the impossible becomes possible. Keep praying, My precious daughter. I am listening, and I am moving.

When Someone You Love Walks Away

Luke 15:20

So he got up and went to his father. But while he was still a long way off, his father saw him and was filled with compassion for him; he ran to his son, threw his arms around him and kissed him.

Romans 8:28

And we know that in all things God works for the good of those who love him, who have been called according to his purpose.

My precious daughter,

I see the ache in your heart when someone you love begins to walk a path that leads them into pain and hardship. I see how deeply this weighs on you, how easy it is to carry their choices in your own heart and wonder what you could have done differently.

I know the questions you wrestle with. Wondering if somehow this reflects on you. Wondering if your love was enough. Wondering how someone you care about so deeply could continue moving further from what is good for them.

Gently, let Me steady you.

This is not your burden to carry. This is their decision and their journey. You cannot fix it, and you were never meant to.

The love you have given was real, and it was not wasted.

What you can do is continue to love them with compassion while also keeping your heart anchored in Me. Pray for them honestly, even when the words feel heavy. I am working in ways you cannot yet see, and I have not stopped moving in their life.

As you love them, keep your boundaries. Do not lose yourself in fear, exhaustion, or the pressure to rescue them. Stay close to Me and let My wisdom guide you.

This is not easy, My child, and I know how much it hurts. But you are not alone in this. I am holding your heart even as I continue reaching for theirs. Rest in that truth. Your love is not wasted. Your prayers are not unheard.

And I am still at work.

Day 68
Faithful in the Waiting

Isaiah 40:31

But those who wait for the Lord shall renew their strength; they shall mount up with wings like eagles; they shall run and not be weary; they shall walk and not faint.

Hebrews 12:11

No discipline seems pleasant at the time, but painful. Later on, however, it produces a harvest of righteousness and peace for those who have been trained by it.

My precious daughter,

I know trusting Me is not always easy, especially when you have been waiting for so long. I see how weary your heart can become when you have prayed, hoped, and held on without yet seeing the answers you long for. But your waiting is not unseen by Me, and it is not wasted.

I am present even in the stillness, working in ways you cannot yet see.

There are moments when I gently correct and guide you, not to discourage you, but to protect you and lead you back to what is true. My correction is never a withdrawal of My love. It is an invitation to grow in wisdom, clarity, and trust.

Courage does not mean you are never afraid. It means you continue walking with Me even when uncertainty presses in, and the road feels long. I see the quiet strength it takes to remain faithful when answers seem delayed, and hope feels fragile.

You are learning how to wait without losing your heart. You are learning how to receive guidance without shame and how to trust Me without becoming hardened by disappointment.

Do not give up, My child. Do not lose heart.

I am with you in the waiting, in the refining, and in the becoming. Even now, I am strengthening you gently and teaching you to rest in My steadiness rather than your own understanding.

My child, trust Me. I am leading you with care, and I will carry you through this season with peace, wisdom, and strength.

Day 69
Encouraged, Not Condemned

Galatians 6:9

Let us not become weary in doing good, for at the proper time we will reap a harvest if we do not give up.

Philippians 1:6

He who began a good work in you will carry it on to completion until the day of Christ Jesus.

My precious daughter,

I see the effort you are putting in, even when no one else notices. I see the discipline it takes to keep going, to choose what is right, to stay steady when it would be easier to fall away.

But I also see how quickly you move past your progress. How you focus on what is not yet finished instead of what has already been done. How you measure yourself by what you lack instead of recognizing how far you have come.

Let Me shift that gently for you. Every step forward matters.

Every moment of self-control, every quiet decision to stay the course, every time you choose growth over what is easy, it is building something within you.

Your effort is not unnoticed. And it is not without reward.

It is not weakness to recognize what is good. It is not pride to acknowledge growth. It is wisdom to see what is taking shape in your life.

I am not standing over you with a list of failures.

I see your faithfulness.

I see your perseverance.

And I say to you, well done.

Let your heart receive that.

My precious child, you are not failing. You are moving forward. And I am pleased with what I see in you.

Changed *From the Inside Out*

Matthew 11:28–29

Come to me, all you who are weary and burdened, and I will give you rest.

2 Corinthians 5:17

If anyone is in Christ, the new creation has come, the old has gone, the new is here.

My precious daughter,

I know how exhausting it can feel to keep trying to change yourself in your own strength. I see the frustration that rises when old thoughts, fears, or patterns seem to linger longer than you hoped they would. But My child, you were never meant to carry the weight of transformation alone.

Come close to Me and let Me gently change you from the inside out.

This is not a change born from pressure, fear, or striving. It is a work shaped through love, truth, and walking with Me day by day. As you remain near to Me, I will begin renewing the places within you that have felt weary, fearful, or stuck for so long.

What once defined you no longer has authority over your life. The shame, fear, and old ways of thinking that kept you bound are not your identity anymore. I am leading you into freedom, clarity, and peace.

As My truth takes root within you, your heart will begin to change. Fear will loosen its hold. Peace will begin to grow where striving once lived.

And through it all, know this: I understand you completely. Nothing about you is hidden from Me, and nothing about you makes Me pull away.

Stay close to Me, My precious child. Even when the change feels slow, I am still making all things new within you, and what I begin in love will continue to grow.

Day 71
Speak Life

Proverbs 18:21

The tongue has the power of life and death, and those who love it will eat its fruit.

2 Corinthians 4:13

It is written, I believed, therefore I have spoken. Since we have that same spirit of faith, we also believe and therefore speak.

My precious daughter,

I hear the words you say to yourself.

The quiet thoughts that move through your day, the ones that say, "I am too much," or "I always mess things up," or "nothing ever works out for me."

Those words are not from Me.

They were never true.

You have learned to speak from hurt and fear, but I am teaching you a different way.

I hear what you have been telling yourself.

Now listen to what I am saying.

You are not too much.

You are deeply loved.

You are not failing.

You are being formed.

Nothing is wasted.

I am working in your life.

It may feel unfamiliar to speak this way about yourself. I understand that. But I am asking you to trust My words until your heart begins to recognize what is true.

Speak what I say.

My precious child, speak what is true.

Day 72
Love Beyond What You Can See

Micah 6:8

Act justly, love mercy, and walk humbly with your God.

1 John 3:17

If anyone has material possessions and sees a brother or sister in need but has no pity on them, how can the love of God be in that person?

My precious daughter,

Not every wound can be seen from the outside. I know how easy it can be to look at someone's words, choices, or behavior and only see the hurt they caused, without seeing the pain they may have carried for far longer than anyone realized.

Many people are living from places within them that were never properly loved, comforted, or healed. Some learned to survive before they ever learned how to feel safe, trusted, or cared for. And when pain is carried for a long time, it often spills into relationships and touches the lives of others.

This does not excuse harm, but it can help you respond with wisdom and compassion instead of bitterness.

Look at others through gentler eyes. Behind many hardened hearts is deep sorrow. Behind anger is often pain. Behind broken behavior is often someone who has gone too long without love.

So when you have the opportunity to offer kindness, patience, or understanding, do not hold it back. Compassion has the power to soften places that judgment cannot reach.

My child, I am teaching you to love with both wisdom and mercy. As My love heals your own heart, it will begin to flow outward into the lives of others.

Do not underestimate what a single act of genuine love can do in a broken heart. Your gentleness and compassion toward others may be the very thing that begins to set them free.

Day 73
When You Stop Performing

1 Samuel 16:7

The Lord does not look at the things people look at. People look at the outward appearance, but the Lord looks at the heart.

Galatians 1:10

Am I now trying to win the approval of human beings, or of God? If I were still trying to please people, I would not be a servant of Christ.

My precious daughter,

I see how tiring it has become trying to carry the expectations of everyone around you. I know how often you have felt the pressure to say the right thing, do the right thing, and become what others needed you to be. Somewhere along the way, you learned to measure your worth by approval, and it left your heart exhausted.

The world may judge you by what they see and hear, but I look within your heart. I see your motives, your intentions, and your deep desire to please Me. I see the quiet faithfulness that others may overlook.

I also see how torn you can feel, trying to meet the expectations of others while longing to remain true to who I have called you to be. Carrying the weight of others' approval is not what I asked of you. That burden will only slow you down and pull you away from the freedom I desire for you.

Let go of the need to be validated by people. Their opinions shift, their expectations change, and their approval is never meant to define you. Release what others think you should be and lean into who I say you already are.

When you release the need for approval and stay close to Me, your heart begins to breathe again. You begin to walk in freedom, clarity, and peace instead of fear and exhaustion.

You are not failing, My precious child. I am guiding you gently, and you are already deeply loved here.

Day 74
Know Your Worth

Psalm 139:14

I praise you because I am fearfully and wonderfully made.

Proverbs 31:25

She is clothed with strength and dignity; she can laugh at the days to come.

My precious daughter,

I know there have been moments when the way others treated you made you question your value. Moments when neglect, harsh words, rejection, or being overlooked slowly wore down your confidence and left you wondering if you were asking for too much simply by wanting to be loved well.

But My child, your worth has never been defined by how others treated you, what they failed to give, or what they took from you. Your value was never placed in human hands to determine.

You deserve love that is steady, respect that is sincere, and relationships that nurture rather than diminish you. I care deeply about the beautiful things I placed within you, and I do not want your heart dimmed by relationships that wound more than they heal.

You do not have to accept less than what reflects My love and care for you.

When you feel unsure or worn down, come back to what is true. Let truth anchor you. Let the wisdom of My values guide you toward what is healthy, honoring, and life-giving. You do not need to accept less than what reflects My love and care for you.

I am shaping you into a woman who walks with strength and grace, who knows her worth, and who no longer settles for what continually harms her heart.

Stand confidently in who you are, My precious child. You are deeply loved, fully worthy of care, and safely held in My unchanging love.

Day 75
Stand in My Truth

Psalm 91:2

I will say of the Lord, 'He is my refuge and my fortress, my God, in whom I trust.'

Psalm 3:3

But you, Lord, are a shield around me, my glory, the One who lifts my head high.

My precious one,

I am your refuge and your fortress.

When lies surround you, when thoughts rise against you, when words spoken by others try to take root in your heart, come to Me. I am your safe place. I am your covering. I am the One who stands between you and what seeks to harm you.

As you trust in Me, I will deliver you. As you hold onto My truth, the lies will begin to lose their power. What once felt overwhelming will begin to fade as you choose to believe what I say instead of what fear or others have spoken.

Let go of the lies that turn you against yourself.

You were never meant to fight yourself. You were never meant to carry thoughts that accuse, tear down, or distort who you are. Those are not from Me. My truth brings clarity, peace, and strength.

I am your shield.

You do not have to defend yourself in your own strength. You do not have to live guarded or afraid of what others may say or think. I am your protection. I am your defender.

You do not need to fear people. Their words only gain weight when you receive them as truth.

Stand firmly in My truth, My precious child. Let My words become the place where your heart rests, steady, protected, and safe in Me.

Day 76
Grace Has the Final Word

Psalm 103:12

As far as the east is from the west, so far has he removed our transgressions from us.

Romans 8:1

Therefore, there is now no condemnation for those who are in Christ Jesus.

My precious daughter,

I know how heavy regret can feel when your mind keeps returning to past mistakes, painful memories, or moments you wish you could undo. I see how easy it is to carry guilt quietly within yourself and to wonder if you have truly been forgiven or if you will always be defined by what happened.

You are forgiven. Let go of the guilt you have been carrying and release the weight that no longer belongs to you. Forgive yourself, and forgive those who have hurt you, not because what happened was right, but because I desire freedom for your heart.

Let My sacrifice free you. What I have done is complete and sufficient. You do not need to keep punishing yourself for what I have already forgiven. Shame does not come from Me. Condemnation has no authority over you.

You are forgiven. Your sins have been cast as far as the east is from the west, never to be held against you again. I do not rehearse your past or define you by your mistakes. I see you through grace, mercy, and love.

So go live in freedom. Remove the shackles of sin, regret, and self-blame. Walk forward unburdened, restored, and made new. What once held you no longer has power over you.

Lift your head. Breathe deeply. Step into the life I have given you. You are deeply loved, My precious child. Walk forward in freedom, and do not return to what I have already released you from.

Day 77
Redeemed, Not Disqualified

Joel 2:25–26

I will repay you for the years the locusts have eaten… You will have plenty to eat, until you are full, and you will praise the name of the Lord your God, who has worked wonders for you.

My precious daughter,

Shame tries to convince you that your past disqualifies you, that what has hurt you or what you regret has the final word over your life. But shame does not speak for Me. What I redeem is no longer marked by failure. It becomes a testimony of My grace, My strength, and My healing at work in you.

Do not try to hide yourself from Me. Do not hide your pain, your hurt, or your disappointment. I already see it all, and I am not turned away by it. When you come to Me honestly and allow us to face these things together, healing begins to take root where shame once lived.

This work we do one-on-one is sacred. It is where strength is formed and where freedom grows. You will not emerge broken or diminished. You will come out stronger, steadier, and more compassionate than before.

One day, you will recognize how I am using your story to lift others who feel unable to raise their heads. You will become a source of comfort to those who believe their past defines them. Through you, they will see that yesterday does not determine today, and that each new day carries hope.

Walk forward without hiding. Your past no longer has authority here. I am redeeming it, and I am leading you into what comes next.

Day 78
What Fire Could Not Destroy

Zechariah 13:9

I will refine them like silver and test them like gold.

Isaiah 43:2

When you walk through the fire, you will not be burned; the flames will not set you ablaze.

My precious daughter,

Stand up.

What you have walked through was hard. There were moments it felt heavier than you could bear. But you are still here. And what once threatened to break you has also strengthened you.

You are stronger now, but not harder. You have been softened, too.

What you have endured has given you deeper compassion, deeper empathy, and a greater awareness of the hearts around you.

This fire was not meant to consume you. It was meant to refine you.

Just as silver is shaped through fire, your life has been formed through the trials you have walked through. And though the process was painful, it has pulled away things that once held you back.

You are becoming wiser. Stronger. More compassionate. More grounded in love.

Your tears will not last forever. One day, they will turn into awe, and then into joy. I am guiding you through every part of this transformation.

So do not stay bowed down in defeat.

My child, rise. And let what you have walked through become a light that helps others find their way, too.

Your Scars Tell a Story

Romans 8:28

And we know that in all things God works for the good of those who love him, who have been called according to his purpose.

Isaiah 61:3

To bestow on them a crown of beauty instead of ashes, the oil of joy instead of mourning, and a garment of praise instead of a spirit of despair.

My precious daughter,

I know there are wounds you still carry quietly. Moments that changed you, pain that left marks on your heart, and battles that took more strength than anyone around you fully realized.

You are a warrior. Not because you have never been wounded, but because you have risen again and again. The battles you have faced have shaped you, and the scars you carry tell a story of endurance, courage, and faith.

Do not hide your wounds. Let them become a source of strength. What once brought pain can now bring wisdom, compassion, and depth. I am teaching you how I redeem suffering and transform what was meant to harm you into something that brings life.

I am a God of restoration. I take broken places and make them whole. I take loss and turn it into purpose. Nothing you have endured has been wasted. I am weaving healing and meaning into every part of your story.

As you walk forward, you will begin to see how pain has been reshaped into strength and how suffering has given way to restoration. Trust Me with what you have survived. I am still at work, and what I am creating is good.

Stand strong. Walk boldly. My love for you has never wavered, My precious child. My presence is always with you.

Day 80
Nothing Was Wasted

Zephaniah 3:17

The Lord your God is with you, the Mighty Warrior who saves. He will take great delight in you, in his love; he will no longer rebuke you, but will rejoice over you with singing.

Isaiah 43:19

See, I am doing a new thing. Now it springs up, do you not perceive it? I am making a way in the wilderness and streams in the wasteland.

My precious daughter,

I delight in you. I rejoice over you with singing and surround you with joy. I am your greatest encourager, lifting your heart when you feel weary and reminding you that you are deeply loved and never forgotten.

I know there have been moments when it felt like what you went through did not make sense. Times when the pain felt unnecessary, when the waiting felt too long, or when you wondered if anything good could come from it. I saw all of it. Nothing you walked through was unseen.

Even when you cannot see it yet, things are shifting. Doors are opening, pathways are being cleared, and breakthroughs are unfolding in ways you may not yet understand. What once felt stuck is beginning to move. What felt delayed is being prepared.

Even what was meant to bring you down, I am turning for your good. Nothing has been wasted. No pain has been overlooked. I am redeeming what was meant to harm you and shaping it into strength, wisdom, and testimony.

Trust My perfect timing. Growth does not always announce itself, and progress is not always loud. Stay faithful. Stay hopeful. Do not give up when the journey feels long. Blessings and favor are coming, not because you forced them, but because I am faithful to fulfill what I have promised.

Rest in My joy. Lean into My encouragement. You are deeply loved, My precious child. My precious child, you are held in My care, now and always.

Day 81
The Courage You Carried

James 1:2–4

Consider it pure joy whenever you face trials of many kinds, because you know that the testing of your faith produces perseverance.

Isaiah 40:31

But those who hope in the Lord will renew their strength. They will soar on wings like eagles; they will run and not grow weary.

My precious daughter,

You are strong. You have faced obstacles that could have stopped you, yet you did not remain where you fell. Even through sleepless nights, moments of doubt, and times when you felt worn down, you stood back up again and again. That strength did not come from nowhere. I formed it in you through perseverance, faith, and courage.

The trials meant to break you have made you stronger. Each challenge refined you, stretched you, and revealed what I placed within you. I have been with you every step of the way, steady and faithful, even when you felt unsure of the road ahead.

There were moments when the future felt uncertain and the outcome unclear, yet you kept moving forward. You did not give up. You trusted, even when trust was difficult. Your perseverance matters. I have seen it, I honor it, and I remember it.

Soon you will see what I have prepared for you. What is coming will reflect My faithfulness and My care. The strength you carry now will make sense in the season ahead.

Walk forward with confidence. Rest in what you have overcome. You are secure in Me, My precious child. What I have placed within you will carry you forward.

Leave Yesterday at the Cross

Isaiah 43:18–19

Forget the former things; do not dwell on the past. See, I am doing a new thing! Now it springs up; do you not perceive it? I am making a way.

My precious daughter,

I know how memories can linger. I know how the pain of your past can surface unexpectedly, pulling you back into moments you wish no longer had power over you. What you have lived through mattered, and it shaped you in ways that were not always gentle. I do not ask you to pretend it did not happen.

Still, I want you to know this: your past does not determine your future. I am doing something new in you. I am not calling you to live in yesterday or to remain bound to what once hurt you. What has been does not get the final word over who you are becoming.

Forgetting former things does not mean denying your story or rushing your healing. It means releasing what no longer serves life. It means choosing not to let old wounds dictate new decisions. I am inviting you to loosen your grip on what was, so you can receive what is unfolding now.

To let go, you will have to leave the past where it belongs, at the cross. Not because it was insignificant, but because I have already carried it for you. I have borne the weight of your pain, your regret, your sorrow, and your questions. You do not need to keep carrying what I have already redeemed.

Come forward with Me. Let yesterday rest. A new beginning is before you, shaped by grace, guided by truth, and held in love. I am with you as you step into it, gently, faithfully, and without fear.

Day 83
Beauty From Ashes

Psalm 56:8

You keep track of all my sorrows. You have collected all my tears in your bottle. You have recorded each one in your book.

Isaiah 61:3

To bestow on them a crown of beauty instead of ashes, the oil of joy instead of mourning, and a garment of praise instead of a spirit of despair.

My precious daughter,

You have walked through things that could have destroyed you. You have endured loss, betrayal, and moments that felt like the very end. I saw every tear you cried, every silent ache you carried, and every prayer you whispered when words were hard to find. None of it was unseen. None of it was forgotten.

Every tear has been kept in My bottle of remembrance. Every sorrow has been counted. What felt like abandonment was never absence. I was with you in every step, holding you, even when you felt alone.

What you thought was the end is only a new beginning. I am not finished with your story. I am a God who restores, redeems, and rebuilds. I take what was broken and shape it into something meaningful and strong.

As you have been comforted, you will now become a comfort to others. The compassion you carry was formed through experience, and I will use it to bring healing and hope. Nothing you have endured has been wasted.

I am turning the broken places into something beautiful. I am exchanging ashes for beauty and sorrow for joy. Trust Me with the process. What is unfolding will reflect My faithfulness.

Rest in My promise. Walk forward with hope. You are deeply loved, My precious child. My presence is always with you.

Day 84
Commit Your Ways to Me

Colossians 3:17

And whatever you do, whether in word or deed, do it all in the name of the Lord Jesus.

James 1:5

If any of you lacks wisdom, you should ask God, who gives generously to all without finding fault.

My precious daughter,

Commit whatever you do to Me. You do not need to separate your spiritual life from the rest of your day. I am present in your work, your conversations, your decisions, and the quiet moments in between. When you invite Me into what feels ordinary, I delight in establishing your path.

I know there are moments when you wonder if what you are doing truly matters, or if the small things go unseen. Nothing is overlooked by Me. Every step taken in trust, no matter how simple, carries meaning and purpose.

I make firm the steps of those who walk with Me, not by removing every uncertainty, but by steadying your heart as you move forward. You do not have to see the whole road to take the next step. As you choose Me again and again, even in small ways, I am guiding you with care.

Whatever you do, whether in word or deed, let it flow from love and trust. When your actions are shaped by My presence, they carry purpose beyond what you can see. No effort is wasted when it is done with a willing heart turned toward Me.

You are not walking through your days unnoticed. I am attentive to every step you take. As you commit your ways to Me, I will continue to direct you, strengthen you, and lead you forward with faithfulness and peace.

Day 85
The Lesson in the Leaving

Romans 8:1

*Therefore, there is now no condemnation for those who are in
Christ Jesus.*

Psalm 32:8

*I will instruct you and teach you in the way you should go; I will
counsel you with my loving eye on you.*

My precious daughter,

There was a season when you tried harder than you should have. You stayed longer and gave more than was required, hoping things would change if you just held on a little more. I know how much effort that took and how deeply you hoped it would be different.

That season was not My plan for you, but it was not wasted. I was not asking you to prove yourself or to endure beyond what was healthy. I was waiting for you to step away, not as a failure, but as an act of wisdom and trust.

Do not feel shame for what you did not yet know. Do not carry anger toward yourself for staying when you believed love, loyalty, or effort might make a difference. You acted with the understanding you had at the time, and I was with you even then.

Let this be a learning experience, not a sentence you continue to serve. Wisdom often arrives through trials, because growth happens when truth becomes clear. You have grown. You are stronger now, not hardened, but wiser.

Most importantly, you have drawn nearer to Me. You listened. You learned. You responded. And that matters more than how long it took to see clearly. I am proud of how you allowed this season to shape you, not define you.

Rest in what has been gained. Walk forward without shame. I am with you, and I am leading you with care and love.

Day 86
Renewed Within

2 Corinthians 4:16

Therefore we do not lose heart. Though outwardly we are wasting away, yet inwardly we are being renewed day by day.

Psalm 73:26

My flesh and my heart may fail, but God is the strength of my heart and my portion forever.

My precious daughter,

I see the changes in your body.

I see the moments when something that once felt easy now feels difficult, when strength feels different, when movement slows, when you notice limits you did not have before.

I know this is not easy.

There are things you once did without thought that now feel just out of reach. And in those moments, it can feel like something is being taken from you.

I see that.

But listen gently to what I am doing.

Even as your body changes, your spirit is being renewed.

There is a strength within you that is not fading. A depth that is growing. A quiet resilience formed through all you have walked through.

You are not becoming less.

You are becoming deeper. There is still purpose here. You do not have to measure your worth by what your body can or cannot do.

I am with you in every step, whether it feels strong or fragile. Your body may change, but My presence does not.

And neither does your worth.

My precious child, stay with Me in this. There is still beauty here.

Day 87
My Presence in Everyday Life

Ecclesiastes 3:12–13

I know that there is nothing better for people than to be happy and to do good while they live. That each of them may eat and drink, and find satisfaction in all their toil — this is the gift of God.

Psalm 118:24

This is the day that the Lord has made; let us rejoice and be glad in it.

My precious daughter,

There will be seasons when nothing dramatic is happening, when life feels quiet and steady rather than intense or demanding. Do not mistake this for absence or stagnation. I am just as present in these moments as I am in the ones filled with urgency or change.

As you grow and mature, your heart will learn to recognize joy in simpler places. In the rhythm of waves meeting the shore. In a bird resting in a tree. In a squirrel darting across the ground. In the unexpected comfort of a familiar voice on the other end of the phone. These are not distractions from life. They are invitations into it.

Faith in these seasons looks like noticing. It looks like gratitude without a reason, trust without urgency, and peace without explanation. You are learning to see Me not only in the extraordinary, but in the ordinary beauty that surrounds you each day.

Let yourself enjoy these moments without wondering what comes next. You do not need to wait for something bigger to feel alive or connected. I am meeting you here, in the stillness, in the simplicity, in the quiet joy that settles gently over your heart.

This, too, is faith. A faith that rests, receives, and recognizes My presence in every small and sacred detail of your day.

Day 88
Uncomplicated Love

Romans 8:38–39

For I am convinced that neither death nor life, neither angels nor demons, neither the present nor the future, nor any powers, neither height nor depth, nor anything else in all creation, will be able to separate us from the love of God that is in Christ Jesus our Lord.

Jeremiah 31:3

The Lord appeared to us in the past, saying: I have loved you with an everlasting love; I have drawn you with unfailing kindness.

My precious daughter,

There is something unique about our love. It is not complicated, unless you make it so.

I am with you at your best. I am with you at your worst.

I am not keeping score of your sins. I meet you exactly where you are.

On your hard days, when everything feels heavy.

On your quiet days, when words feel unnecessary.

On the days you feel you have nothing left to give.

I am there. Steady. Present. Unchanging.

In a world that shifts and changes, I do not.

You do not have to earn your way back to Me.

You do not have to fix yourself before you come close.

You are already welcomed here.

I am your refuge in every moment, through the storms and through the stillness. You are not facing any part of your day alone.

What we share is not rushed or fragile. It is built over time, through trust, through honesty, through every moment you have come to Me just as you are.

These moments matter.

They are not small to Me. They are where our connection grows. My child, stay with Me in this simple place.

You are known here. You are loved here. You are safe here.

Day 89
The Gift of Today

Psalm 118:24

This is the day that the Lord has made; let us rejoice and be glad in it.

Matthew 6:26

Look at the birds of the air; they do not sow or reap or store away in barns, and yet your heavenly Father feeds them.

My precious daughter,

There is a quiet goodness woven into your days that is easy to overlook if you are always waiting for something more. I invite you to receive this day as a gift. This moment, this breath, this ordinary rhythm of life is not insignificant to Me. I am present here, just as I am in seasons of change or struggle.

I delight when you find satisfaction in the simple things, in your work, in shared meals, in small accomplishments, in rest at the end of the day. These are not lesser blessings. They are gifts meant to be enjoyed, not rushed through. Joy does not always arrive with celebration. Sometimes it comes quietly, settling gently into your heart.

Rejoice in today. Not because everything is perfect, but because I am with you in it. Each day holds its own grace, its own beauty, its own opportunity to notice My care. You do not need to wait for tomorrow to be grateful.

Look around you. Just as I care for the birds of the air, I am attentive to you. I know your needs, your worries, and your hopes. You are held by the same faithful love that sustains all of creation.

Let your faith be steady here, in the ordinary, in the simple, in the gift of this day. I am near, providing, sustaining, and inviting you to live fully in the quiet goodness I have placed before you.

Day 90
Rooted in What I Have Spoken

Isaiah 26:3

You will keep in perfect peace those whose minds are steadfast, because they trust in you.

Jeremiah 29:11

For I know the plans I have for you, declares the Lord, plans to prosper you and not to harm you, plans to give you hope and a future.

My precious daughter,

When fear speaks loudly, remember that I am your peace. Fear does
not have authority over you, and it does not get to decide how you live
or who you become. Let My peace steady your heart and quiet the
noise around you.

When life feels empty or uncertain, remember that I created you with
purpose. Your value is not diminished by seasons of waiting or
moments of confusion. Even when you cannot see what lies ahead,
your life is held with intention and meaning.

When you feel alone, remember this truth. I will never leave you. My
presence does not fade when circumstances change or when others
step away. I remain constant, faithful, and near.

Let what I have spoken about you become the foundation of your
identity. Do not allow fear, loss, or disappointment to shape how you
see yourself. You are defined by My love, My truth, and My promises.

Stand firm in who you are in Me. Circumstances may shift, but My
word over your life does not. You are held, you are known, and you are
never alone.

Day 91
Come to Me First

Matthew 6:33

But seek first his kingdom and his righteousness, and all these things will be given to you as well.

Matthew 11:28

Come to me, all you who are weary and burdened, and I will give you rest.

My precious daughter,

I want you to come to Me not as a last resort, but as a meaningful relationship. I do not desire to be the one you reach for only when everything else has failed. I long to walk with you from the beginning, sharing your questions, your hopes, and your daily decisions.

When you come to Me, you are not admitting defeat. You are declaring surrender. Surrender is not weakness. It is trust. It is choosing relationship over control and faith over fear. When you surrender your heart to Me, you make room for My presence to move freely in your life.

As you place your trust in Me, I am able to shift what feels immovable. I can intervene where you feel stuck. I can quiet what feels overwhelming and bring clarity where confusion remains. I am not limited by what unfolds naturally. I am at work beyond what you can see.

Let our relationship be the place you begin, not the place you arrive after exhaustion. Come to Me freely, honestly, and often. I am ready to meet you there, to walk with you, and to guide you with love and care every step of the way.

Day 92
A Listening Heart

1 Kings 19:11–12

The Lord was not in the wind, not in the earthquake, not in the fire. And after the fire came a gentle whisper.

Psalm 46:10

Be still, and know that I am God.

My precious daughter,

There is no fear here, only My presence. Slow your steps and trust Me. I am inviting you into a posture of listening, not rushing, not hardening yourself, not distracting your heart with things that do not matter.

A listening soul is not a weak soul. It is a disciplined one. It is restrained, attentive, and wise. Listening shapes you. It steadies you. It helps guide you in the way you should go. When you listen before you speak and observe before you judge, you make room for love to lead.

Do not harden your heart when things feel overwhelming or unclear. Do not numb yourself with noise or busyness. Instead, remain open. I am speaking, often in quiet ways. My whisper is gentle, and it requires you to slow down enough to hear it.

I hear the cries of the oppressed, the whispers of the broken, and even the unspoken needs of My children. I am always speaking, but for you to hear Me, it requires you to be humble. It requires patience. It asks you to pause rather than run ahead, to stay present rather than rush past what I am doing.

Stay close to Me. Let your heart be soft and teachable. Trust that as you listen, I am guiding you. You do not need to hurry to be led well. Walk with Me, and I will show you the way.

Day 93
What Truly Matters

1 Corinthians 14:33

For God is not a God of disorder but of peace.

Matthew 6:33

But seek first his kingdom and his righteousness, and all these things will be given to you as well.

My precious daughter,

I see how pulled you feel. Like you cannot finish one thought before another demands your attention. Like, no matter how much you do, something is still left undone. Like everyone needs something from you, and there is little left for yourself.

It feels like you are always behind. Like you are trying to hold too much at once.

I see it all.

But I was never the author of confusion. I am a God of peace, order, and purpose.

You were not created to carry everything. You do not have to respond to every demand. You do not have to meet every expectation.

You are allowed to stop.

You are allowed to say no.

Your value is not found in how much you can hold together.

Come closer, and let Me show you what truly matters. I will help you sort what is important from what is simply noise. Some things feel urgent, but they are not yours to carry.

When you place your life in My hands, I will guide you. I will show you where to give your energy. As you walk with Me, the pressure will begin to lift, and clarity will take its place.

Let Me order your days, not by demand, but by peace.

My precious child, you do not have to carry it all.

Day 94
What Fills Your Heart

Jeremiah 2:13

My people have committed two sins: They have forsaken me, the spring of living water, and have dug their own cisterns, broken cisterns that cannot hold water.

Psalm 16:11

You make known to me the path of life; you will fill me with joy in your presence, with eternal pleasures at your right hand.

My precious daughter,

What you set your heart on will shape your life.

I see the places where desire begins to pull at you, where something starts to feel like it will finally satisfy, finally bring peace, finally make you feel secure.

But when your heart is set on what cannot truly fill you, it begins to demand more from you than it was ever meant to.

It asks for your time. Your energy. Your attention. And still, it leaves you wanting.

You may find yourself striving, reaching, trying to keep up, hoping that the next step, the next achievement, or the next possession will finally quiet what you feel inside.

But it does not because it was never meant to.

Nothing outside of Me can fill what I created within you.

I am the one your heart is searching for.

When you come to Me, when you spend time in My presence, when you slow down and allow your heart to rest, something begins to shift.

The striving eases. The pressure lifts. The emptiness fades.

You were not created to chase what cannot satisfy you. You were created to live from a place of fullness.

My child, come back to Me. Walk with Me. Spend time with Me, and in the beauty I have placed around you. This is where your heart is filled. This is where peace remains.

Day 95
You Do Not Have to Fight This Way

Deuteronomy 20:4

For the Lord your God is the one who goes with you to fight for you against your enemies to give you victory.

1 Peter 5:8

Be alert and of sober mind. Your enemy, the devil, prowls around like a roaring lion looking for someone to devour.

My precious daughter,

I see how long you have been fighting.

The way you stay ready, always braced for what might come next. The way you feel like you have to defend yourself because it has not felt safe not to.

And now you are tired.

Tired of carrying every conflict.

Tired of always being on guard.

I see that weariness.

But you do not have to keep fighting this way.

You are not alone in the battle.

I go with you, and I fight for you.

Not every battle requires your response. Some things are meant to be released into My hands, not carried in yours.

Let Me be your defender.

When you feel pulled into conflict, pause and come to Me. I will show you when to stand and when to step back. I will lead you in peace.

You are safe with Me.

Lay down what you have been carrying.

My precious child, you do not have to fight alone.

Day 96
Calling Lived Out Daily

Micah 6:8

He has shown you, O mortal, what is good. And what does the Lord require of you? To act justly and to love mercy and to walk humbly with your God.

Mark 10:45

For even the Son of Man did not come to be served, but to serve, and to give his life as a ransom for many.

My precious daughter,

Many people believe that calling is only found in ministry or in visible roles, but calling is revealed in everyday life. It is seen in how you carry yourself, how you treat others, and how you respond when no one is watching. Your calling unfolds quietly through obedience, humility, and love.

You reflect My heart when you choose to be supportive, protective, and willing to stand in the gap for others. When you help the weak, listen with compassion, and show patience, you are living out your purpose. This is how I walked among you. I did not come to be served, but to serve, and I invite you to follow Me in the same way.

Readiness for your calling is not marked by pride or striving for more. It is revealed when you no longer feel the need to prove yourself. You have learned to work in partnership, to walk humbly, and to obey with a willing heart. You honor relationships, you value others, and you choose love over recognition.

This is the soil where purpose grows. Continue to walk faithfully in these quiet places. I see every act of humility and every choice to serve, and I am pleased with how you are becoming who I created you to be.

Day 97
Seeds You Cannot See

Galatians 6:9

Let us not become weary in doing good, for at the proper time we will reap a harvest if we do not give up.

Matthew 6:20

Store up for yourselves treasures in heaven, where moths and vermin do not destroy.

My precious daughter,

I know there are moments when you wonder if your life truly has meaning, if what you do matters, and if you are making an impact on the world and the people around you. I see those questions, and I want you to know that your life is full of purpose, even when you cannot see the results.

Everyone in your life is there for a reason. Every conversation, every quiet act of kindness, every word of wisdom or encouragement carries weight beyond what you can measure. You may never know all the lives you have touched on this side of eternity, but nothing given in love is ever wasted.

As you reach out with compassion, patience, and truth, you are speaking into the hearts of others. You are planting seeds that grow in ways unseen, shaping lives in moments you may not remember. What feels ordinary to you often becomes significant in the lives of others.

You are building the kingdom, even when there is no applause, no recognition, and no visible reward. Much of what I do through you will not be fully revealed until eternity, but it is no less real now. Trust that your faithfulness matters.

Continue to love well. Continue to give freely. What you do in My name echoes far beyond this moment. My love for you has never wavered, My precious child. My presence is always with you.

Day 98
Walk With Me Today

2 Timothy 1:6–7

For this reason, I remind you to fan into flame the gift of God, which is in you... For God has not given us a spirit of fear, but of power, love, and a sound mind.

Proverbs 3:5–6

Trust in the Lord with all your heart and lean not on your own understanding; in all your ways acknowledge him, and he will make your paths straight.

My precious daughter,

Walk with Me today. Let My love and My power guide your steps. You do not need to have everything figured out before you move forward. Simply stay close to Me, and I will lead you one step at a time.

Do not hide the gift I have placed inside of you. I formed it with purpose and intention. Do not allow uncertainty or insecurity to silence what I have entrusted to you. What I placed within you was meant to be shared, nurtured, and allowed to grow.

When doubt tries to rise, remember that My strength is made known through your willingness, not your perfection. You are not required to be fearless. You are invited to be faithful. As you walk with Me, courage will come.

Trust My leading today. Let My love steady your heart and My power move through you. What you carry matters, and I will help you use it well.

Walk forward with confidence. You are held in a love that does not change, My precious child. My presence is always with you.

Day 99
Not by Might, but by My Spirit

Zechariah 4:6

Not by might nor by power, but by my Spirit, says the Lord Almighty.

Romans 12:2

Do not conform to the pattern of this world, but be transformed by the renewing of your mind. Then you will be able to test and approve what God's will is.

My precious daughter,

I have not called you to live as the world lives, striving in your own strength or measuring your worth by outcomes and timelines. I have called you to walk in trust, rely on Me, and let My Spirit lead you.

You were never meant to carry this life in your own strength. You were created to walk in partnership with Me. When you try to manage everything on your own, it becomes heavy. But when you surrender and allow Me to lead, what once felt overwhelming begins to settle into peace.

What I am doing in your life is not accomplished by might or by power, but by My Spirit. When you feel tired or uncertain, remember that you are not carrying this alone. I am at work beyond what you can see, moving in ways that do not depend on your effort.

There will be moments when you are tempted to rely on your own strength, to push harder, or to control what only I can carry. In those moments, return to Me. Let go of striving. Choose trust. I will steady you and guide you in ways formed through relationship.

Do not conform to the patterns around you or compare your journey to others. As your mind is renewed, you will begin to see more clearly what I am doing and why My ways are different. My pace is not rushed, and My work is not incomplete.

When the time is right, I will bring to life what I have placed within you. You do not need to force what I have already planned. Remain close to Me. Rely on Me. I am faithful, and I will fulfill what I have spoken.

Stand Firm in the Authority I Have Given You

Ephesians 6:10–11

Be strong in the Lord and in His mighty power. Put on the full armor of God, so that you can take your stand against the devil's schemes.

Luke 10:19

I have given you authority to trample on snakes and scorpions and to overcome all the power of the enemy; nothing will harm you.

My precious daughter,

Stand firm in the authority I have given you. You are not standing on your own strength or wisdom. You stand in My name, clothed in My power and upheld by My truth. When you remain rooted in Me, nothing meant to shake you can prevail.

There will be moments when opposition rises or when pressure tries to cause you to retreat. In those moments, remember who you belong to and who goes before you. I have equipped you with everything you need to stand steady and unmoved.

Spiritual authority is not loud or forceful. It is calm, confident, and grounded in trust. It comes from knowing My Word, walking in obedience, and refusing to be swayed by fear or doubt. When you stand firm in Me, darkness has no power over you.

Do not shrink back when challenges appear. You are called to stand. As you stand in faith, I fight on your behalf. As you remain anchored in truth, I surround you with My protection.

You have been given authority to overcome, not by striving, but by abiding in Me. When you speak My truth, walk in love, and refuse to compromise what I have placed in your heart, you reflect My strength to the world around you.

Hold your ground, My daughter. Keep your eyes fixed on Me. Let My Word be your foundation, and My presence be your confidence. You are not easily shaken because you are firmly planted in Me.

A Blessing as You Go Forward

My precious daughter,

I bless you as you go forward from this place.

I bless the journey you have walked, every step of healing, every moment of surrender, every quiet choice to trust Me when it was not easy. Nothing has been wasted. Everything has been held with care, and it has all been used to shape you into who you are becoming.

I bless your heart with peace that does not depend on circumstances, but rests securely in who I am. When life feels uncertain, may that peace steady you. When the path feels unclear, may it guide you gently forward.

I bless your mind with clarity. May you discern what is true, what is right, and what is worth your time and energy. May distractions fall away, and may your thoughts remain anchored in truth and wisdom.

I bless your voice. May your words bring life, healing, and encouragement. May what you speak reflect love, strength, and grace, both to others and to yourself.

I bless your steps. May you walk with intention, not striving, but trusting. May you move forward with courage, knowing you do not walk alone. I am guiding you, strengthening you, and leading you in ways you will continue to discover.

I bless your calling. What I have placed within you is not small, and it is not accidental. As you live your life, may you reflect My light in ways that reach further than you can see. May your faithfulness bear fruit, even when it is unseen.

I bless your future. It is not uncertain to Me. I am already there, preparing, aligning, and unfolding what is good. You are not behind. You are not forgotten. You are being led with purpose and care.

Go forward in peace.

Go forward in confidence.

Go forward in the truth of who you are in Me.

You are chosen.

You are strengthened.

You are held.

And you are deeply loved.

Walk with Me, My daughter. There is more ahead.

Numbers 6:24–26

The Lord bless you and keep you;
the Lord make his face shine on you and be gracious to you;
the Lord turn his face toward you and give you peace.

Final Blessing

My precious daughter,

You have walked through these pages, and I have been with you in every word.

I have seen the places where your heart softened, where truth began to settle more deeply within you, and where hope quietly took root again. Nothing you have experienced here has been by accident. I have been drawing you closer, reminding you of who you are and how deeply you are loved.

Carry this with you.

When life feels uncertain, remember My nearness.

When doubt begins to rise, return to My truth.

When you feel weary, rest in My presence.

You do not leave this time with Me, you continue walking with Me.

I go before you.

I walk beside you.

I remain within you.

There is more ahead, more growth, more healing, more purpose, more of My love unfolding in your life. You do not need to strive for it. Simply stay close to Me, and I will lead you.

You are not the same as when you began.

You are stronger.

You are steadier.

You are more deeply rooted in truth.

And you are still becoming.

Walk forward with confidence, not in yourself, but in Me. Trust what I am doing, even when you cannot see it yet. I am faithful to complete what I have started in you.

You are My daughter.

You are held.

You are loved.

Always.

A Note Before You Go

Dear reader,

If these letters have brought comfort, healing, or a fresh awareness of God's love to your heart, would you consider sharing that with another woman who may need to hear it too?

A short, honest review helps this devotional reach the hands of someone who is searching for hope, perhaps a woman who feels unseen, weary, or unsure of her worth. Your words may be the very thing that leads her to open these pages and discover how deeply she is loved by her Heavenly Father.

It only takes a moment, and it means more than you know.

Scan the QR code below to leave a review.

https://www.amazon.com/review/create-review/?asin=1972179640

Thank you for being part of this journey. May the Lord continue to bless you, draw you near to His heart, and remind you each day that you are His precious daughter.

With love and gratitude,

Stacy Huddleston